BLACKBIRD MEDLEY

The Transformation of a Gangster

STAN LONG

Copyright © 2011 by Stan Long. All Rights Reserved.

In memory of,

Lamar Finch, Keith Joyner, Heartbeat, Lil Tye, and all of the hommies that I've lost in the struggle. May God bless all of your families.

In special memory of,

Georgianna Medley, my grandmother who I lost years ago. You were the glue that held us together. The angels are smiling around you. I will never let all of your hard work be in vain. We all miss you and you are irreplaceable.

Special Thanks

Lelia Leverette (mom), for having to put up with all of the painful situations that I put you through. I can't change the past, but I will try to bless you with a better future. God is great and you taught me that, and He has changed my heart like you said He would. I'm not perfect but I'm better. Thank you for being the best mother I could have asked for in the world.

Extra Thanks

Janaee, I know we have had our ups and downs but through it all you still believed in me. Thank you so much for holding me down when I needed you the most. You were there during a critical time in my life and I will always love you for the sacrifices you made for me. (RELLO)

Terraye Starr of Majestic Web and Graphic Designs, you have been a great friend and also a great help in making my first book a success. Thanks for all that you do. I will never forget you.

Crystal Baptiste, thanks so much for being down for me and helping me in the clutch. You have a heart of gold. I can't say enough about you.

Shout outs to:

My son, you are the driving force of my life. Your daddy loves you and I always will.

John McCants, you have always been real with me from day one.

Big Jeff, you are like my brother and I'm down with you for life.

Everyone from the whole DMV (DC, MARYLAND, VA) area that's on their grind.

Special thanks to Carla of CAM Talent Management your assistance on this project was priceless. You'll find her on Twitter: @supermomanger

I see you:

Jay-Z, you kept all the real dudes on their toes for years. I appreciate you for making real music for the gangstas. Oh yeah, you didn't have to do it because I got rid of that dirt for them in Maryland. LOL

Russell Simmons, I watch everything you do and you're a hard act to follow. Thank you for giving us vision.

India Arie, the music you give us is heartfelt. The conversation we had at Houston's I never forgot.

President Barack Obama, thanks for raising the bar for all black men. You made us dream again.

Monique, you have inspired so many women around the world. Your energy is amazing and thanks for giving people like myself a platform for success.

Steve Harvey, I thank God for you because you show the world that you can confess to not be perfect but still love God. I see God blessing your life so much because you acknowledge Him.

Wale, thanks for putting DMV on the map worldwide with hip-hop.

Michael Baisden, you're not afraid to talk about the real topics in radio and we thank you for it.

Contents

Introduction

Chapter 1   My Childhood

Chapter 2   Coming of Age

Chapter 3   The Making of a Boss

Chapter 4   Becoming Heavy in the Game

Chapter 5   The Death of Skinny

Chapter 6   The Transformation of a Gangster

Chapter 7   Going to Atlanta and Meeting Peaches

Introduction

I'm sitting at the counter in my condo, staring into the granite patterns and reminiscing about my life. I stand up to face the mirror to get a clear view of the pain that shows on my face. I can't believe after all the drug dealing, fancy cars, clothes, women, and all-out fast living, I find myself here. As I look at the man before me in the mirror, standing at five foot seven, 175 pounds, dark skinned with a clean-shaven head, I still can't see past the pain of being in the fight of my life. I suit up in Hugo Boss to get ready for court, and I think of all the things a man could find himself in court for; this one just never came to mind. They say God doesn't put more on you than you can handle. I try to hold on to that thought as I wonder how I got here. Maybe this is karma for all the wrong I've done. Maybe womanizing and living selfishly have finally caught up with me. All I know for sure is that I wouldn't wish this on anyone, not even my worst enemy. They say lots of men find themselves in this position, but I never dreamed it would be me, this time I feel like I'm in a mental prison before even arriving at court. To make matters worse, my lawyer told me that the judge is a real bitch.

The thought of taking the biggest loss of my life has consumed me daily. My friends and family have tried to keep me in good spirits, but even they realize that this time I might have stepped in some real shit. I guess this time only God can save me from what I'm about to face. I'm a soldier, so I'm staying strong, but I can see how this could break a man down. Before I go any further, I should tell you a little about myself ...

Chapter 1
My Childhood

I was born in Halifax, Virginia, on February 16, 1968. This was a time when the world didn't look very promising for young blacks—or even old blacks for that matter. At that time, black leaders were being killed off as soon as they could be heard. I always wondered how this negative energy would affect my life.

My mother, Lelia Long, was a young eighteen-year-old with big dreams. My father was young as well, with lots of ambition. They were newly married with a fresh start on life, but it was not such a happy time. My father was very abusive both verbally and physically. He never had a relationship with his dad, so maybe this was the reason for his anger. He told my mother he would never leave his son the way his dad had left him at a young age, and Mom gave him the benefit of the doubt. This would later prove to be not such a wise decision. They say you have to see a man to be a man. My father was a hard worker, but as for family life, well, that's where the trouble started.

My father moved from Virginia to Washington DC in the hope of creating a better life for his new family. He received a job offer at a printing company shortly after his arrival. My mother then left me with my grandmother in Virginia, joined my father, and tried to find work. Now, in my mind, my grandmother was the strongest woman alive. She had raised seven kids and what seemed like a hundred grandkids. She was the glue that held the family together. She made sure we all had what we needed, which was difficult to do on a farmer's salary. She would work at white folks' homes doing house chores and wiping piss or whatever it took. She also had a few acres of tobacco to be farmed. That's where having lots of grandkids paid off. She was a very stern but loving woman. She was definitely not having it. She looked after me until it was time for me to join my parents in DC. I was still an infant at the time.

When I arrived in DC, riots were tearing the city apart because one of the most powerful leaders, Dr. Martin Luther King, had just been assassinated. Blacks were not allowed to enjoy the same liberties as whites even though we were free. Things were bleak in the streets, and inside our home, to make matters worse; my father started accusing my mother of cheating and took her wedding ring away. That was just the beginning. My father told my mother to leave and go back to Virginia, so she and I returned to my grandmother's home. This would not be the last of the breakups. Rather, it was the beginning of me moving from place to place with no stability. My mom did all she could, but if you think it's hard being a single parent now, picture being a young, black, single mom in 1969.

There wasn't much hope for blacks in the South at the time, so my uncle asked us to move to New York with him. My uncle Johnny had six children, so there was never a dull moment from the moment we arrived. Soon, Mom got a job as a phone operator. In those days, a phone operator was more like a switchboard operator.

One day while at work, my mother got a call that changed her life forever. It was from a young, white man trying to place a call to his parents. My mother placed the call and said, "You have a collect call from Brad." The father answered the phone and said he was not accepting a call from any "nigger operator." The boy said, "Dad, stop it," and the call was accepted. It was then that Mom realized she needed to go to school so that she could get a better job. So again, we moved back to Virginia, and Mom enrolled in Southeastern Business College in Durham, North Carolina. You can probably guess where that left me—with grandma. It was less than two hours from Grandma's house to the college, but we were so poor that Grandma couldn't afford a bus ticket for Mom to come home to see me on the weekends. However, they did manage to find enough money for a visit once or twice a month. I was always so happy to see my mom. She lived in a dorm and was the only girl with a child, so all the girls would rant and rave over me when I arrived that made me feel special. Mom finished the course she was taking in only one year, graduating in 1971.

When I was almost two years old, she was offered a job with the FBI in DC after having the highest scores on a placement test. During this period, my mom and dad were working things out and soon reconciled. My father left McArdle Printing Company in DC and was hired at Bethlehem Steel in Baltimore. We moved in with my father's family. Things were starting to look up at last. My mother did not except the FBI job because she had to be at work too early for me to be at a daycare. Shortly after, we moved into project housing called Park Heights Terrace. These were really bad apartments, but they were affordable. My mother soon took a position with the Social Security Administration (Black Lung Center) in Woodlawn, Maryland. I was finally put in daycare. So my mom was a GS-3 clerk-typist, and my dad was an indoor crane operator. His salary was four times my mom's, but he still insisted on making her pay half of all the bills.

Eventually, the physical and mental abuse started up again. My dad would become jealous and go into rages and become physical. It got so bad that Mom left and took me back to Virginia to Grandma's house. We stayed for a short time until Mom faced the harsh reality that it was a dead end living in Virginia. We soon moved back to Baltimore, to Utah Street—tall row houses in a drug-infested neighborhood. It was a very rough hood with shootings on a regular basis. She took a job at Poole and Kent, a mechanical contracting company. My father could not accept the fact that she had moved on with her life, so he continued to harass my mom. Her first day on the job, Mom got into her car to go to work and soon found that Dad had pulled all the wires from the hood. Fluid ran out all over the ground, and Mom couldn't go to work that day. We were having really bad times.

One day, my grandmother visited us. When she saw where we lived, she cried and begged my mom to move because it was so bad. She also asked if she could take me home with her. My mom was the only woman in the building, but for some reason (God) the drug addicts and drunks were never anything but nice to her. Once again, Mom decided to move—this time to a duplex on Garrison Boulevard. It was a much better area, but the duplex wasn't the best. She couldn't lock the front door, so she would prop a chair against it. Mom had rough times, but you'd never know it based on her loving, caring ways. She was always in good spirits. Mom became good at hiding her pain.

I was getting older, so now Mom wanted me to be back with her. My grandmother asked her to go to live with her sister who also lived in Baltimore not far from where Mom was living on Garrison. So Mom and I moved in with Aunt Ola on Popular Grove Avenue. I was now old enough to know what was going on. Things were looking better, and I was happy. Aunt Ola had a niece and nephew, Daryl and Cindy, living with her. That made it more fun for me. After a while, Mom had trouble with Aunt Ola because she wanted money all the time. You can guess what happened next; we moved again, this time into a one bedroom on Dennison Street. It was another duplex but in a nicer neighborhood. It was actually the nicest place we had lived in so far, so things were really starting to look better in my eyes. I was around six years old at the time. Although I had to share a room with Mom, it still felt like heaven to be in a safe environment. Mom and I began to bond and do things together because we were finally living under the same roof for a long period of time.

My father and mother were now separated, and he was ordered to pay child support, thirty dollars a month. You can't really call that support even in those days. Sadly enough, he didn't want to pay, so the court had to take it out of his check. Now Mom qualified for subsidized housing because of her income, so after a year on Dennison, we moved to a place called Winchester Arms Apartments. This had two bedrooms and was a fairly new place, so I felt we had hit the lottery. For the first time, I had my own room. The apartment we had was on the second floor facing the elementary school I was to attend. I was so excited that I begged Mom to let me stay home that day to help move in. She agreed, and I jumped for joy. This place turned out to be the one that shaped me as a child. One thing that stands out in my mind is that it was the only place we had lived in that had a garbage disposal. I couldn't wait to tell my first-grade teacher. When I did, she told me never to put my hand in it because it would cut off my fingers. I was a very talkative child, so my teacher knew all my business as well as my mom and dad's.

My mom had gotten a divorce by this time, so my father made it clear that if they weren't together, he wasn't having anything to do with me. Remember his promise never to leave me the way his father left him. Well Lee Owen Long did just what he promised not to do. I would wait outside for him when he said he was on the way, but he would never show up. My friends gave me a hard time about it, so I eventually stopped waiting.

I quickly made many friends and became very popular. People started coming to my house to see if I wanted to come out to play. Before long, I had friends all over the area and started playing sports. I became involved with Little League baseball and was very good. I also played Pop Warner football. Living in the projects is a challenge, and you learn to protect yourself quickly. I remember my first big fight was with a boy named Mark. He tried to take my ice cream money. I was small, but I wasn't a sucker. He found that out the hard way. We fought in front of my whole hood. I must have hit him with everything in me. I quickly gained respect in my hood. Kev, Donnell, and his brother Erry were my best friends. Now Kev, he was the pretty boy with curly hair and light skin. Donnell was quite the opposite. Erry was a jokester and liked to start trouble. But together we were inseparable. We all played sports and did well.

Meanwhile, Mom was working in downtown Baltimore as a secretary at an army recruiting office. Soon after, she took a job on the DC side of Maryland at Andrews Air Force Base. This is when I started to get into trouble. She didn't get home till late, so I was home alone most of the time. Now my friends were older than me by a few years and knew trouble well. I was a fast learner, so it didn't take long for me to catch on. One day, my friends came to get me and said, "Let's go have fun." Not knowing what they had in mind, I was down. We ended up on some train tracks (Amtrak).

"When the train comes, let's throw rocks at the passengers and run," said Kev.

"We'll ambush their ass," Erry said. I remember the rocks being so big, we could barely lift them. So along came the train, and we began the rocks throwing. We were cracking windows left and right. We began to run, and as soon as we thought we had gotten away, we slowed down. Before we knew it, the police were right in our faces with three police cars.

"Get on the ground!" they screamed. I was as nervous as a hooker in church.

One of the officers asked why we were throwing rocks. "We didn't throw any rocks. We're on our way to the store for my mom," said Kev.

"Some boys just ran past us; maybe they threw the rocks," said Erry.

The officers asked our names and then let us go. My heart was in my sock. That was my first encounter with the law, but it would not be the last. My friends were use to trouble, but this was new for me. My mom didn't play when it came down to it, and I knew it.

My friends and I would sometimes go to other neighborhoods because they had a recreation center—a "rec." Next to one rec was a train track with freight cars. It was around June, and Mr. Jones from the rec center told us that the freight cars had fireworks on them. "Let's hop the freight cars to find out," said Kev. So we did. We climbed aboard the train and saw crates with fireworks in them.

"Throw the fuckin' crates off, and we can pick them up when the train passes," said Erry.

We did just that, and as Donnell climbed off, I heard, "Oh shit." His pants had gotten caught on the train and he couldn't get off.

"Take your fuckin' pants off," said Erry. So Donnell did and then jumped off in his underwear. After laughing a long time, we stashed the crates and went home. Donnell walked all the way home in his underwear.

"Dumbass, you could have gotten your foot cut off the way your ass was hanging," I said. "Y'all thought that shit was funny," said Donnell. "I could've gotten killed."

This was how we made our fun. So because of this type of behavior, Mom started sending me to the country with Grandma for the summer.

My uncle Ice was staying at my grandmother's at that time. He was more like a father to me than an uncle. He was also a real gangsta, and I knew it. He could gamble well, and I didn't know all that he did, but I knew he always had money. He started teaching me things I never thought you could learn in the country. I must have been about eight or nine when he said "Come on; let me show you how to shoot a gun. That way you can go hunting with me." So he handed me a .38-caliber handgun and took me into the woods. "Hold your arms out," he said. And then with the gun pointed straight forward, he placed his hands over mine and stood behind me. "Now pull the trigger once you have your aim," he said. *Bang!* The gun went off and I almost shit in my clothes. This didn't seem right for someone my age, but I sure felt gangsta. We repeated the exercise until I was no longer afraid. Little did I know what this would lead to.

My uncle was a great guy but a little misguided to say the least. In his eyes, he was making me a man. He played softball on a league team, so he often took me along. One time, he said, "Take my keys and go to the store for sodas for the team." I could barely see over the wheel at that time, but what kid wouldn't want to drive a car? "Listen to me," he said, "if you crash the car, just get out and run and I'll report the car stolen." Now as a child, it all made sense, but looking back, what if I got into a head-on collision, ran into a ditch, or flipped the damn car over? Since it was my uncle, I trusted what he said. God was with me, so I made it back safely. My biggest fear was whether or not I had gotten the right sodas.

Sometimes my uncle would take me to craps games with him. He'd say, "Want to make some money?" What kid doesn't? "I need you to hold the light, and every round they're going to have to pay you," he'd explain. I would come home with $100 or more every time. Having money that young gave me a swagger. I felt like a big boy and really looked up to my uncle. He was the only real man in my life and taught me all the rules of manhood. He said never to be a snitch. He would say that there are consequences to everything in life and that you need to know them. As a child, these things went over my head, but I never forgot them. "Don't let your mouth write a check that your ass can't cash," he would say. *Why the hell are you telling this to a ten-year-old?* I thought to myself. Later these things would prove valuable.

He was so gangsta that he would leave the car running and just go. "What if someone takes it?" I would ask.

His reply was, "I wish a muthafucka would."

On the off days, my uncle would take me with him to work for white farmers with big crops. They didn't want me to help because I was so young. "I'll make sure he doesn't get behind," my uncle would tell the boss. He would pull his row fast to help catch up my row, and they would pay us $12 a day. That's right, I said *day*—not hour. I took the money to pay for my own school clothes. Mom could only afford Bobo's and Tough skins. I had my new swag, so those clothes didn't work anymore.

I was getting used to going to the country and spending time with my uncle every summer. Mom continued to send me to my grandmother's because I wasn't behaving in school. Then in the summer of 1981, Mom hit me with some bad news. "I have a new job and we have to move to Philly," she said.

I didn't want to go to Philly. "I'm tired of moving. We're worse than gypsies," I said. "Stan, this is so we can live better. One day you'll understand," she said. She was right, but it wasn't that day—that's for sure.

I had a feeling I knew why we were moving. After my father, I had never seen my mom with a man, and then Chester came over one day. Mom introduced him as a man from church, and I started seeing more and more of him till it was time to move. For some reason, I felt as if he was the reason we were moving.

One day, before we moved, a neighborhood friend named Goo and I decided to go out looking for money with a new flashlight mom had given me. We searched the whole field and found nothing. Goo and I decided to give up on the hunt and go in since it was late. "Let's check under the steps before we go in the house," I said. Now under these steps was piss and trash—you know, project shit. We looked anyway, and I couldn't believe my eyes. It was a knot big enough to choke a horse. It was wrapped around a bag of dope. I thought it was fake because it was so much and I had never seen that much money in my life. I ran in the house to show Mom. She took the money and kicked us out of the room. Goo and I sat in my room thinking of all the things we could buy. After all, we were rich now—or so I thought. It turned out to be about ten thousand dollars. We gave Goo some and kept the rest. It was the happiest day of my life at the time. Little did I know it was the icing on the cake; now we were moving for sure. Chester and Mom had been dating for a while, but something went wrong and we were out.

When we left Maryland, I was very sad. My friends all cried, and so did I. I started thinking about all the times we had on Winchester Street—like when we played Hide and Go Get It. This was a game we played with the "faster" girls of the neighborhood.

The girls would hide, and then when we found them, we got to hump them with our clothes on. This one girl, Kendra, who was the neighborhood freak, got caught by Goo. "I told Kendra to take off her clothes. Man that shit smelled like piss" said Goo.

"Did you get some?" I asked.

"Hell no! I wouldn't hit that with your dick. Kendra smells like she pissed on herself." From that day on, we called her little pissy.

Then there was this time when it snowed so much it covered the cars in the street. "I know how we can make some money," said Erry.

"Another bright-ass money idea," said Kev.

"No, I'm dead serious. This shit will work," Erry said. "Let's go to the corner store and break in and loot. They can't call the police on us."

"That's the stupidest shit I ever heard. What're we going to steal? Some Now and Laters?" Kev said.

"No, dumbass, we're going to steal cigarettes and sell them. We can keep the candy for ourselves," Erry explained.

"Now that's a plan," said Kev. So we went to the corner store and found out that everyone had the same plan. When we arrived at the store, people were coming in and out with bags of stuff. The only cigarettes left were on the floor from people dropping them.

"Your plan is a little late," I said to Erry. We started picking stuff up off the floor, whatever we found that people had dropped. We had candy for days and not much else, but it was fun at the time. The National Guard finally came around in Jeeps with snow chains and chased people from the store. For once, we were long gone before they arrived.

On moving day, I also thought about the rec that had finally been built in our neighborhood. It was for the whole area, but I felt like it was just for my hood because we ran it. We were popular, so everyone knew us from Winchester Arms. One man in particular, Mr. Boyd, paid close attention to us—or should I say me. He had something to say about everything I did. One day, I asked him why he was so hard on me and not everyone else. He looked at me and said, "Because you're not everyone else, Stan. You have something special. One day you're going to be somebody." It didn't register in my mind at the time, but later, he and everything he said would come back to me. He was one of the first positive men in my life. He would single me out and correct me all the time. I thought he was picking on me, but now I know he was only trying to make me live up to my potential. He would say I could be anything I wanted to be. He saw I was good in sports, so he pushed me even harder. One day, just like most days, he said, "Stan, how are your grades coming?"

"I don't need grades, I need to be playing sports," I said.

He laughed and then turned to me with a look I hadn't seen before. "Who the hell's team are you going to play on with bad grades?" he said. "In case you don't know, you have to have a certain grade average to play on a team, Stan."

"Not if you're really good," I said.

"Who told you that?" he asked with a strange expression on his face.

"Kev told me," I said.

"If he hasn't played on a team, then how does he know what it takes to be on one?" That was how all of our conversations went. He was like a father figure. After we moved, I never saw Mr. Boyd again, but I think about his words even today.

The day we moved, I also reminisced about the school I would be leaving. I used to sell candy to the kids in school to make a little change. One day, I had a fight with a boy from another neighborhood in school. Okay, it wasn't a fight. When he approached me, Donnell, Kev, and Erry saw him and walked up. I swung at the boy, and so did they. He was mad because I didn't want to sell him candy. I would only sell to kids I knew because I could trust that they wouldn't tell on me. After we jumped the boy, he went right to the principal and told on me for selling candy. They raided my locker, and that was the end of the candy selling. I got suspended for three days.

Another memory that will stick with me for life is my second-grade teacher, Mrs. Billingsly. She was a very pretty lady, but that wasn't what I thought about. I would sit and stare at her feet all day. She moved my desk up front because I was very talkative. I was so glad because that way I could look right at her feet with a clear view. One day, she was teaching and I was looking down at her feet. "What are you looking at, Stan?" she said.

"Mrs. Billingsly, you have pretty french-fry feet," I said. She laughed so hard that I was embarrassed.

After she stopped laughing, she said, "Thank you, but Stan, you have to pay attention." We were all very poor in my hood, and we all wanted a change badly. We talked about nice things other kids from other neighborhoods had. We would go to the county and take Mongoose bikes from kids and ride them home. I couldn't keep my bike because Mom would have killed me if she found out. One of the last memories I had of Winchester Arms was the time we all were playing basketball in the parking lot. We were doing the regular things we always did when all of a sudden—*bang, bang, bang.* We turned to run and—*bang,* another shot. We saw a man in the parking lot holding a gun. He had just shot his cheating girlfriend in the head right in front of us all. Then as we ran, we hear a last *bang*; he shot himself in the head. I very seldom had a chance to see role models where I lived.

    I remember admiring a guy named Mr. Brother. Now this guy had money, or so I thought. He lived in the building next to me and had a daughter named Kim who wore only rabbit coats and things like that. Mr. Brother had a swag that was different. He had two Cadillac's and always had on something new. He had lots of women, pretty women. This was not the everyday project man. We all knew he was doing something wrong, but we all wanted to be him. He would give us all money when he saw us at the ice-cream truck. His daughter, Kim, was older, maybe sixteen at the time. She loved me like a little brother, and to her girls, I was her little boyfriend. I wished it was true.

    Now we had this new start in Philly. We were there for only a short time, but I recall we lived on Pine Street. Summer came, and again I was off to the South. Mom was engaged to a guy in Philly who was an old friend of hers. I was informed that after the summer, when I returned, it was going to be to Delaware. Claymont, Delaware, was like a foreign country. I didn't think I would like it at all, but surprisingly enough, I loved it. I met some great friends like Dorian and Will from Connecticut. I got into music and started practicing being a DJ. This was big at that time, and Doo Wop was a popular mixed tape DJ. This is when I first heard mixing music on the radio. I was starting to get interested in girls too, and I was the new kid in school, so all the girls wanted to get with me. They said I was cute, dark, and chocolate. This was a surprise to me because in Maryland, you had to be light skinned with curly hair for them to find you attractive. I was glad to be getting all the attention and quickly became a playboy. I hadn't had real sex yet, but I thought I knew it all.

My friend Will was from Connecticut, so he was more city. He had an older sister who had graduated. One day, she said, "Take your pants down."

I said, "What if Will comes in?"

"Don't trip. I can hear him," she said. So I took my pants down, and she put her hand in my underwear and began to do something that felt great. I had never had this happen and I didn't want her to stop. I didn't know at the time that I was being molested. This went on for about six months. She started going further by telling me to meet her in the Laundromat. She came in one day with a dress and no underwear on. She said, "I want you to fuck me today." I was afraid because I was a virgin. "Don't tell anyone about this," she said. I promised I wouldn't, and she lifted her dress and lay on the floor. "Lay on top of me," she said. I was so scared; she had to tell me to take off my underwear. Finally I did, and she put me on top of her and told me to kiss her tits. She started getting excited. Then she said, "Put it in now." My heart was pounding, but I did as I was told. I quickly had an orgasm, and she got mad. I thought it was great, but she thought it was too quick. From that day on, I tried to date many girls. I thought it was cool to have sex so young. Mom never talked about sex, so I learned in the hood. Girls liked me, so this didn't help the situation. I would sneak girls home from school to have sex. I even encouraged my friends, Dorian and Will, to bring girls over. Will had no idea that his sister, Tanya, had been teaching me how have sex. I became a lot more involved with girls than most kids my age. I didn't even realize that it was wrong at the time. My name began to get out as the fast boy who would actually have sex and not be scared.

I met this one girl named Jocelyn who I liked a lot. She wasn't a fast girl and was more appealing to me. Her father was a pilot, so he was never home. Her mom wasn't in her life, so I would always go to her house after school. One day I said I wasn't coming over but then ended up going over there anyway. She came to the door and immediately started getting mad at me for coming over. She wouldn't let me in. I forced my way in only to find my best friend, Dorian, on the sofa. I was crushed because I thought she was a good girl. I said, "Is this who you want to be with?"

She started crying and said, "No."

"I'm sorry," Dorian said as he left. He asked to talk to me outside.

"What the fuck is this?" I asked.

"Man, I didn't touch her, but you're dogging this good girl out Stan," he said. "She's too good for that." He went on. We exchanged words, but at the end of the day, we were still best friends. He was right about what he had said, but it wasn't his business. We had time away from each other to air out, but before long, we were back playing football and basketball and hanging out. A short time later, I decided that Jocelyn couldn't be trusted and left her alone. I soon was back to my player ways.

Just when the fun was really starting, Mom got a job offer in Maryland as an Equal Employment Opportunity Specialist, time to move—again. I was getting older, so making friends was becoming more difficult. Mom said she was only trying to make our lives better. At the time, I was convinced that she was doing the very opposite. I was fourteen years old and growing up fast. This was when my life started to take a really bad turn.

Chapter 2
Coming of Age

I quickly learned that the DC side of Maryland was very different from any other place I had lived. They did things fast and early. Even the music was different from what I was used to. They loved go-go music like Chuck Brown, Rare Essence, and Junkyard. I soon caught on and started to like it as well. We were living in an apartment that was across the street from the school I was to attend. At first, it was difficult for me because the dress code was so different. The area had a style of its own. Actually the people there had a lifestyle all their own. I quickly adapted and started making new friends.

One of my new friends was a guy from DC name Elliott. We all called him Black because he was just that. Something about him made me curious. He had a swag that was different from the Maryland side. He was somewhat serious and yet funny. He dressed differently with his Levis and New Balances. He also carried a briefcase all the time instead of the normal book bag. I quickly had a few altercations, and Black witnessed one of them. He saw that I wasn't afraid of anyone and was okay with my hands. This also got me noticed with the ladies. Black lived in my new neighborhood, so we started to hang out.

Black and I began going to the basketball courts at the school across the street, and that's where I met others in the hood. Three people started to become friendly with me and wanted me to play on the same team as them. I had skills, so I guess that was why. Black wasn't good at all, so he was optional. Dell, Count, and Derrick were already friends and had lived in the hood for years. Sometimes I noticed that Dell seemed a little jealous and didn't want me around. He was a boxer and was used to getting all the attention. Me being the new kid on the block may have taken some of that away. Black didn't like them much. He said to me one day, "Stan, why do you hang around them bammas?" *Bamma* meant "country" or "slow" or something of that nature.

"Nah, they're all right," I said.

"Shit, these bammas aren't about making money. They're just a bunch of mama's boys. Go with me to the city and I'll show you what's up," he said. Black lived with his older brother because his mom and dad were dead. "I'm not a fuckin' mama's boy. All I got is me out here. That's why I'm all about my money. Fuck these clowns. Let me show you how to get money," Black said.

That sounded good to me because we were barely making ends meet and I wanted to make money. The lifestyle that my uncle had introduced me to was now coming into play. "Let's go to the city so you can show me what's up," I said.

Black took me to his house and then called some female to pick us up. "I'm going to show you some shit. You better not tell a fuckin' soul. I don't let any of these muthafuckas in my business around here," he said. Black went into his closet and pulled out a trash bag full of weed.

"Where did you get all that shit from?" I said.

"This ain't shit! I have a connect for as much as I want; I be moving this shit like candy in the city. I'm from Edgewood," he said. Now it started to make more sense why he was able to dress so well. Black started to roll up a joint. "You want to hit this shit before we leave?"

"Nah, I'm good," I said.

"You never smoked before, have you," he asked.

"No, but I've been around it."

"That's good that you don't smoke because this way you can make more money. Once you start smoking, it takes away from a lot of stuff," he said.

"Well then, why the hell are you smoking?" I said.

"Muthafucka, if you lost your mother and father, you'd probably be smoking too. If I didn't smoke dis shit, I'd go crazy out here. Me and my brother don't even get along. I'm hustling to survive out here, man. I want to get the fuck out of this place. My brother be stealing money from me and taking my weed," he said. "Come on, let's go to the city. Our ride is here." A pretty, older chick came in, and I soon found out that she was his girl. She said not one word to me as I got in the car. They talked little as we drove into DC, and then she dropped us off on a corner down the street from some apartments. "This area's a little hot. Never get dropped off in the middle of a hot spot. Everybody around here sells something. Mainly we all sell weed. The older dudes are selling coke," Black said.

Now I was thinking, *what have I gotten myself into?* We walked up a hill, and Black went into the woods to stash some of his weed. We stayed up on the plaza for about an hour, and he must have sold about a pound. As time passed, it started slowing down. "I just wanted you to see how I get down. It's slow today because it's the middle of the week. I just wanted you to watch my back and see how it goes," said Black. I was amazed at what I had witnessed. I had never seen anything like it before. It was like a drug factory. Cars pulled up and handed him money; he handed them drugs, and they left.

"Man, I've never seen no shit like this before. You don't think the police can drive up and catch you?" I asked?

"We all watch out for each other, and when they come, the youngins will tell us by yelling 'Jo Jo's'. We have a system and we all follow the rules. You have to stick together in order to win. Let's go because I need to count this money. You don't want to have a lot of money and drugs on you at the same time," he said.

I didn't know it at the time, but I had just been introduced to the hustle game. Sadly enough, it felt good to me; Black had power and respect because he had money. Older guys even gave him respect. He had this older girlfriend picking him up and dropping him off. I was really drawn in and this day would prove to be only the beginning. We made it back to Maryland, and Black asked, "So what do you think? Is this something you could do?"

With no hesitation, I answered, "Hell yeah!"

"Okay then, I'll put you down and we'll get this money together," he said.

At the time, I didn't realize how this would affect my life. I had been raised with morals and taught to have respect. This was not the life I had envisioned for myself, I guess the money and a chance for a better lifestyle drew me in fast. I continued to play with other kids from the neighborhood, but things started to look different in my eyes. I longed more and more to be this big shot that would be envied. After all, I had come from nothing and I saw a chance to be accepted as successful. I had never realized until that day with Black that everything that my uncle taught me growing up would be the making of a gangster. Selling drugs in those days were taboo it was not openly discussed, and you were viewed as a very bad person. My school days continued, and I started to meet more and more people. My days of going to Edgewood Apartments also continued. The people in my school started to view me differently. My dress code quickly changed because the money started to come. I had to hide my clothes from Mom so she wouldn't see the change. Somehow my mother always figured me out. I started meeting people at school that were also involved in drug sells. My cousin Pat lived in Glenarden Apartments, where a lot of drugs were being sold. I met other guys who lived around Glenarden and started to hang out there.

One day, Black said, "Man, have you ever been to the Go-Go?"

"Nah, not yet, but I wouldn't mine going," I said.

"Okay, then I'm going to take you," he said. So one Friday, we all met up at Edgewood and left to go to the Go-Go. At this time, the Go-Go was mainly for real thugs who hung out in what we called crews. You may consider them gangs, but we really didn't. We were just a group of boys who represented our neighborhood. Now at the Go-Go you had a chance to represent your neighborhood as the band played. This was a new experience for me. Fights would break out constantly because of the different hoods not getting along. For some reason, I fell quickly in love with the Go-Go. I guess it gave me a sense of belonging. I hadn't had that feeling because of moving so often from place to place.

Years went by and we still lived in the same area. I had lots of friends, and most of them never knew I was selling drugs. I had made many friends in DC and Maryland. My Maryland friends rarely wanted to hang out in DC with me, probably because it was so fast paced. During one of the times at the Go-Go, I met a boy named Go-Go Rock. He was from DC and could dance his ass off—hence his name, Go-Go Rock. We all got along—me, him,

Black, and some others from Edgewood. He was from Southeast DC, which was like Brooklyn and the Bronx all rolled into one, nothing but projects and crime. Drugs were sold over on this side at an alarming rate, but if you didn't live in Southeast, you didn't hustle in Southeast.

I got a job as a stay-in-school worker, as a supply clerk at The Dept. of Agriculture so now I could start showing money. I quickly bought my first car, a Toyota Corolla SR5. I paid cash, about $3,500. Now I could go without needing to be picked up or asking to use Mom's car. I really thought I was the ladies' man. I was still a pretty regular guy and very funny, so girls were attracted to me. I never had a big head, so girls never thought I sold drugs. If they asked, I would lie and say no. I tried to hide it as much as possible because inside I was embarrassed about it.

I started dating this really cute girl at DuVal High named Niecy. She was nice and she was a virgin. Of course I was a fast ass, so this was a problem. One day she came over and I tried to get her to have sex with me. "Take off your clothes and let's play," I said.

"Boy, I'm not messing with you. I'm not ready for sex," she said.

I started to kiss her and take off her clothes at the same time. "I'm going to take my time, so don't worry," I said. She allowed me to take off all her clothes. I was thinking to myself, *this is it, I got her now*. "Just let me put the tip in," I said. She agreed as I continued to kiss on her breast.

"Wait, wait," she said. "This is hurting me. I don't think I can do it. Maybe we're moving a little too fast."

"I don't think we are. This is what boyfriends and girlfriends do. Don't do this to me—we're almost there, so just relax," I said. This went on for maybe ten minutes with more wait and stops. Finally I gave up and said I would just wait. I tried not to show it, but I was mad as shit because I felt I had waited long enough. I was used to girls being ready and willing. Needless to say, this relationship didn't last long. It was too much of a challenge.

The promiscuous lifestyle was one that I had adopted by now. From Delaware until now, I had been involved with a lot of girls, some even much older than I was. Two girls, Kara and Kim, lived across the hall. Kara was the older of the two. One day, my mom asked her to keep an eye on the house because she wasn't going to be home until very late. I went over to Kara and Kim's place. Kim, the younger sister, had a crush on me. I, on the other hand, had a crush on Kara. "I want you to date my little sister. She's afraid to tell you, but she likes you," Kara said. "Have you had sex before? Cause she's a virgin!"

"No, I'm still a virgin," I lied. What came next shocked the hell out of me. She told me that she wanted to teach me how to have sex so I would know how to break her sister in properly, of course I was all for this. Kara told me to start coming over after school so she could show me a thing or two. Weeks went by and I never showed up because I was going around Glenarden to hustle. One day after school, she knocked on the door, when I opened the door; she was waving for me to come over. I went over, and she took me into her room. She immediately started to undress and took off my clothes. I have to say, I was nervous as shit. She played with herself in front of me for a while. This was all new to me. She then pulled me on top of her and placed me inside of her. Before she said anything, she was riding me like crazy. She started to make noises and that got me so excited, so you can guess what happened next. I had not learned about dick control, so she got mad and explained to me that I was to wait for her. In my mind, I had already waited too long. This continued for some time, and she even started to talk to her boyfriend on the phone while she rode me. She pretended to be having phone sex, finally she said I was ready for her sister but I didn't want her sister at that point and I didn't want another virgin. I had met another girl named Shelly at a fair, and I had started to like her. She was pretty and had really long hair. She attended a rival school called Eleanor Roosevelt High. Martin Lawrence and Alonzo Mourning went there at the time. She later became my prom date.

By the time I had reached the twelfth grade, my hustle game was getting bigger, and I kept meeting other hustlers and they would expand my game. I met a Nigerian named Placy; he owned an auto parts store in Maryland that was connected to a car wash. One day while getting my car washed, he started a conversation with me. At the time, I had jewelry on, which probably told him I was into something. We talked and exchanged numbers, and then he said he was going to help me become more legit. I always wanted to do legitimate business so we became friends and that's when I find out he was also selling drugs. He started giving me drugs for the low. This really enhanced my game. Before then, I was only involved with weed, but PCP was getting really big. This hallucinating drug—water, as it was called—was sold in one-ounce bottles. When mixed with weed and smoked, it took you to a whole other level. Glenarden was selling this drug a hundred miles per hour, meaning really fast. Edgewood, on the other hand, was a weed spot so now I was connected to weed and water.

Things were really taking off. This was around the time that I received the news that brought me to my knees. I was on the phone with a girl when suddenly my mom screamed out, "No! No! Not my mother!" I knew right away that something was wrong. I went to comfort her and found that my grandmother had died while on the phone with my mother. Life as I knew it seemed to just stop and I was completely numb. My grandmother had been the strongest of the family. She was the glue that held us together. I suddenly started playing back many lessons that she had taught. Grandma would say things like, "Stay away from those pissy girls and get your books; you'll have plenty of time for girls." She told me, "Never mind what a person says, watch what they do." These and many other words played over and over in my mind.

We went to Virginia for the funeral. The wind was blowing on that day, and things seemed extremely calm. Everyone was quiet but sad and nothing seemed the same as before. My chest was tight with pain as I tried to hold back the tears. I had never felt this type of pain in my life. Mom was a wreck, and I tried to be strong for her, but when we put my grandmother into the ground, some part of me died with her. It was a feeling I never could explain. She had helped raise me, and once again, I felt that someone I loved had left me. My mom was really involved with Chester, who by now had become her husband. He was starting to have a lot of influence on her decisions. I felt like I had lost my best friend; Mom and I had always been close up until then. I felt that he wanted to put distance between us, because he didn't have a close relationship with his own children, so that must have played a part.

Although Mom often disciplined me, we had more of a sister-brother relationship. After all, it had been just the two of us for us so long. She started saying things to me like, "God said the husband and wife before the child." I knew that was her husband talking. Then Mom started to find things that spelled out drug dealer. She asked where I got my money and how I could afford certain things; I would just lie. Soon, I felt her slowly distancing herself from me. One day, Chester and I had gotten into an argument, and my mom said I had to get out. This was what he wanted all along. He knew my mom loved God, so he used that, saying God wanted this or that. Mom gave me more time to stay there but not much, I knew I had to get my own place.

I graduated from DuVal High School in 1986, and Mom didn't attend because she was in California on a job assignment. To Chester's credit, he was there. My real father didn't show up even after I told him he didn't have to buy me anything. Instead, he took my graduation invitation and sent it to the child support bureau. That's where I had to draw the line I have had enough from him. *I feel alone, so why not just be alone?* I thought. I was saving money, so I told Mom to just give me two weeks and then I would be out. The Nigerian put an apartment in his name for me, and I was out two weeks after graduation.

Now I have to fly or die, I thought to myself. I even got a job working for the government at Harry Diamond Lab. I had worked different jobs in the government, as mentioned earlier; I had worked in the stay-in-school program. As a senior, I only had three classes and then went to work downtown at the Department of Agriculture. I may have sold drugs, but I always worked a regular job too; I wanted to be low-key, and I didn't want to glorify the street life. I even made the guys who worked for me get regular jobs or go to school. The less hot they were, the less hot I was. My uncle always said, "Don't be a show-off because the loudest one is the weakest."

Now I was on my own and life was pretty good. I decided to buy myself a BMW 325. It made me feel like I was doing big things, but I still kept my Toyota Corolla to ride around and do my dirt in. Now girls were all over me because if you had a nice car, you had all the girls. Girls that didn't give me the time of day started to show interest in me. I was strictly about my money, so if we were in a movie and my pager went off, it was time to leave. Selling drugs on a high-end level is very demanding; you don't have a lot of leisure time. I was always looking for another neighborhood to sell in or recruit.

One day, Go-Go Rock called me all excited and said we needed to hook up I went to pick him up, and he told me that his uncle, Big Tone, was getting out of jail tomorrow. "This muthafucka gets money," he said. "I can't wait for you to meet him." The next day, he called again and Big Tone was with him. "Come over to the house and meet my uncle," he said. I immediately went over. His uncle was a very large man and seemed a little intimidating. He appeared to be someone who didn't take shit from anyone.

"Are you ready to make some real money, young boy?" he said. "My nephew says that you do well for yourself. I'm putting my team together because I have a water connect."

At first I was hesitant because I was already making money and didn't need any help.
"So what kind of numbers do you have on the water?" I asked.

"I can give you a gallon of water for six thousand if you pay upfront," he said.

That sent shocks through my body because I was only getting sixteen ounces at a time. I was paying $2,500 for that. One gallon was selling for at least $10,000 on the streets. Without showing too much excitement, I said with a straight face, "Let's get money!" This was the beginning of me getting real money. Now the guy who I got the water from before was all of a sudden buying water from me. I was selling water to everybody and all the older guys came to me to buy it. I also had a weed connect, so

Big Tone got his weed from me. Instead of five or ten pounds a week, I was now selling about twenty-five pounds a week. The game had totally changed.

Big Tone wasn't your everyday hustler who had a lot of rules, and you had to follow the rules in order to play in his game. He told me when we first hooked up that he had no plans to go back to jail ever again. He sat me down one-on-one and made me hear him out. "This game you're playing is a dangerous game; you must play with rules and respect. Never carry drugs on you unless it's necessary. If it becomes necessary, then carry them only from A to B; don't make any other stops. Always stay in a lot of traffic if you're going to make a big transaction. This means early morning or evening rush hour. Keep your registration and license handy and never panic. Do not bring but one girl around your business and don't show her anything. Girls talk too much and will get you killed or arrested. You're only as strong as your weakest link. If a guy is weak, don't sell to him. We're a family and everyone else is a worker. Treat them that way and don't be friendly to the help. If you befriend them, they'll take advantage of your friendship. Trust not one muthafucka in this business; they're all crooks. All hustlers are out for themselves. If you get pinched, don't say shit and someone will come to get you. Do you have any questions?" he said. I said that I didn't. "Good, because if you did, then this shit is not for you," he said. "Stan, I like your style because you don't depend on me or no one to make your way. You're not like my sorry-ass nephews. If not for me, these niggas would drown out here. They didn't do shit while I was locked up. You were making money on your own when I met you. That says a lot about your character. I'm going to take you under my wing."

After all that had been said, I felt like it was my uncle Ice talking to me all over again. A lot of his rules were the same. He talked to me like the father I never had, although deep inside I knew that he needed my ass. I was the strongest hustler on his team. Somehow I felt that we needed each other. He started introducing me to the finer things in life. He taught me to drink the best—Remy Martin VSOP was his favorite. He wouldn't let me mix it with anything. He said real men drink it straight with no chaser. On special occasions, he would buy a bottle of Louis XIII at $1,300 a bottle. When I found out the cost, I almost didn't want to drink the shit. He always wanted me to hang out, just the two of us. We would go down to Georgetown to shop. He taught me about linen and how to dress up. He taught me about gator shoes and the difference between the belly and tail. I didn't really give a fuck at the time, but I listened anyway. He loved to brag to me about what he paid for this and that.

Big Tone became a father figure to me. He was a man's man, and I had a lot of respect for him. On Christmas, we would buy a U-Haul full of trees and give them away in the hoods we sold drugs in. It was our way of giving back. If someone was getting put out, Big Tone would pay their rent. I thought he was crazy because everyone came to him for help, but he said, "You always want to keep the hood on your side." If he met a woman with a pretty daughter, he would say he wanted her to meet his son. He had no children at the time, so I guess I was like a son. Big Tone was about thirty-four when we met. He would buy fancy cars but would never put any rims on them. He often would trade cars with a woman and let her keep his car. This was to stay low-key, he would say. Plus if you got caught with anything in someone else's car, they had to let you go. As smart as he was, he could have been a lawyer instead of a drug dealer. Money came in bunches, and we were living the life. We all had money and nice cars, and I started to get into jewelry. I got a diamond teardrop-shaped pendent with a Gucci link chain. I had a bracelet with four karats worth of diamonds. We knew we were getting more money, so we didn't mind spending it. We would go to Atlantic City and throw money around on the craps table. Everywhere we went, we got the royal treatment. It made me feel like a real big shot. I bought nice furniture and made my apartment look really nice. Girls couldn't believe the way I was living at such a young age. Mom, on the other hand, was embarrassed and couldn't face her friends. Some of them knew me and couldn't believe what I had turned into. I didn't understand why she looked at things the way she did until she reminded me of one of the many incidents that she knew about.

    This guy that Go-Go Rock introduced me to, named Ron, became a good friend of mine, at least I thought so at the time. I was on the way home to my mother's house at the time and got a call from Ron. I hadn't heard from him in a few months because he owed me money. He said he had my money and told me to meet him at the corner store by my mom's house. I was still living with mom at the time. My instincts told me not to go, but I went against them, hoping to get the money he owed me. I got to the store, parked, got out, and then Ron walked up. "What's up, nigga? Why haven't you called me?" Ron said.

    "You know why I didn't call your ass. You owe me, that's why," I said.

    "Man, I told you I would pay you." He started walking and said, "Let's go across the street." I knew something was wrong. He said he was going to his car to get the money.

    Two guys started walking up to us right then. One of them had on a long coat and said to me, "Homeboy, give me a light."

As soon as he spoke, I started to run. He pulled out a sawed-off shotgun. "Stop running or I'll shoot you in your back," he said.

The other guy ran up on me with a handgun. "Why the fuck you run?" he yelled. Then he told me to move to the side of the building. Once I was on the side, he tried to go in my pockets. He hit me in my forehead with the butt of the gun, splitting my head wide open. Then as I wiped the blood from my eyes, I saw him cock the gun and point at my face.

"Freeze!" the police said just at that moment. I hadn't heard them come, but I was sure glad to see them for once. I knew it was God—how else could they have arrived right at that exact moment? They laid me on the ground and asked for a number of a loved one or guardian. Mom was there in five minutes. She saw me with my shirt tied around my head to hold the blood. She never forgot that.

Chapter 3
The Making of a Boss

I was blessed to be alive, and I could hear my grandmother's voice warning me to get off of that path. She always told me not to disappoint her. I really didn't want to be a drug dealer; I just wanted a better life for myself and the people around me. It seemed as though I was groomed to be in that lifestyle.

At this point, Black started hanging with his girl more and hustling less. He was still my man, but we were heading in two separate directions. I wasn't hanging on strips anymore because I was becoming a boss. I handed out work, and that was all I had to do now. Cars started becoming a major part of my life. I traded my 325 for a 528 BMW. We always paid cash for all of our cars. We went out to Virginia to the nice lots that were independently owned. They wouldn't report us.

One day, Big Tone said he wanted me to do him a favor and pick up this young kid for him. He said, "I used to date his mom, and he's coming home from Boys Village." Boys Village was like a juvenile jail for youth offenders. This was a favor that would definitely change my life forever. I was the youngest of the crew, so this became my assignment. Keedie was his name, and he stood about 5'10" and weighed about 210. I thought he was going to be a little boy; I was totally wrong. He was young but not a little boy at all. "What's up, man? You must be big Tony's man. That nigga told me you were going to pick me up. I'm ready to make some money," he said. I wasn't ready to be a babysitter, and he was too young to hang with me, so I took him to Big Tone and we all went out to eat. Big Tone told him all that was going on, and he was ready to go. He was a red dude with green eyes, so I didn't trust him at first. He seemed a lot older than just fifteen, especially streetwise.

Big Tone took him to get a fake ID the next day. "Now he can get in anywhere you take him," said Tony.

Keedie became very cool with me, and we started hanging out. I started fronting him work, and he would finish it the same day. I was amazed at how fast he was pumping the drugs. He was from East Gate in Southeast DC. This was drug heaven and very, very dangerous. Surprisingly, Keedie had many friends, and they respected him a lot, especially considering his age. In fact, I thought they gave him too much respect. I wanted to know how he had gained so much respect at such a young age. I soon found. Some guy owed him money in the hood, so Keedie walked up and hit the guy with a bat and then went in his pocket and took the money. That's when I understood; he was a nut case in the making. For some reason, I liked him more after that. I started teaching him everything Big Tone had taught me. He respected me and did everything I asked him to do. "Man, nigga, you're like a brother to me. I'm glad Big Tone hooked us up ... you're my right hand and if anything happens then I got your back," he said.

Black hadn't been around for quite some time now. We hadn't even been talking on the phone. I thought it was because he was busy. One day, he showed up at my door and I was surprised. He said he heard I was doing good and just wanted to say what's up. We talked for a while and he said he was making money and had moved and gotten a new place. "Let me hop in the shower and then I'll give you a ride home," I said after we had caught up. I hopped in the shower and when I got out, I started talking loudly to Black. He didn't answer. I came out of the bathroom in a towel, and he was nowhere to be found. My front door was cracked, so I went outside to look for him. He wasn't there. Finally I went back into my apartment and started looking around. I noticed that the $900 dollars that was on my dresser was gone. I wasn't mad because, after all, Black had put me in the game. I was more hurt than anything else; I couldn't believe that Black would steal from me. I knew something must have been wrong, so I called my man Cuppy from Edgewood, and he said Black had gotten with some girl and started smoking woolies (crack sprinkled on weed). This leads straight to crack smoking. I was very disappointed because I thought Black was much stronger than that. I called Black a few times, but he never answered. I never saw him or heard from him again.

Keedie, Tony, and I continued to hang out, and Big Tone turned me on to a new hood In DC. "Come on, youngster, I want to show you some new money; we're gonna take over this spot and it's a gold mine. This young kid is running the spot and he's going to be working for you," Big Tone said.

"Who is this new kid and how do you know him?" I asked. "I don't think we should be dealing with anyone new. We're making money and this might make us hot." Big Tone said it was a low-key spot. This guy wasn't getting much water, so I was to be his new connect. Big Tone didn't want him to get into our family because he was going to want a discount. I told Big Tone that this kid Sean could cop from me, but I would set the price. He agreed and then hooked us up. Now Sean was cool and was also about his money. He had lots of guns and lots of workers, but you're only as strong as your connect. He had another spot on another street that was also making money. This meant that I could get to all of this new money through Sean. Now Sean was over six feet tall, 250 pounds, and loose cannon. He was smart though, and he knew that violence and making money don't mix. From time to time, all of us would hang out—me, Keedie, Sean, Tony, and sometimes Bo. We had this family thing going, and for once I felt like I was part of something big.

I was now a general or young boss of my click. I made sure everything went smoothly while Big Tone ran around with girls. I had this girl who was at Bowie State and she had many girlfriends (fly girls) who were all about having fun. She had this one girlfriend in particular that Big Tone was dying to meet. Her name was Evonna and she was a smoking ass chick (good looking). I told Big Tone to pay me $500 and I would hook them up together. He was much older, but Evonna was about money and I knew that. Now of course he went for it and they started hanging out a lot. I would hang out with them too from time to time.

Keedie never wanted to hang out much because he was always in the hood grinding (hustling). He was making money faster and faster, and he was starting to become very popular because he loved to show off. He would shop a lot, so he wore new clothes almost daily. He started wearing jewelry a lot—and nice jewelry at that. Keedie would tell me that he wanted everyone to know his name. He wanted to be a celebrity in the hoods.

It wasn't long before his wish came true. A few years went by, and then Keedie started buying cars—all of them candy-apple red so that people would recognize him. He started hanging out all over the city. We would go to the clubs, and everyone would come up to shake his hand. This muthafucka started thinking he was The Tony Montana of DC. He got a big head, and soon we heard his name involved in all types of shit. So I decided we needed to call a meeting. I went to Keedie's place and we sat and talked. "You can't keep doing this hot shit that you're doing, man. You're going to get all of us locked up trying to be fuckin' famous. If you want to continue getting money, you have to be more low-key," I said. He listened but didn't seem too happy about the talk. Before, it was just PCP or water that we were involved in, but now things were about to change. Keedie explained how he respected my views but didn't think he was being hot at all.

"My name is only in shit because these niggas are hatin' on me," he said.

"Exactly. That's why they'll get your ass locked up, because of the hate," I explained. "Come on, bring your young ass and let's go eat," I said. We went to my favorite spot, a restaurant called Houston's. We often went there to discuss new business. We would always get a table in the back where it was empty. "I met this New York mothafucka named Cookie and he had great numbers on some cocaine. We need to switch up our game and try this shit out," I told Keedie. "He's going to get with me tomorrow, and I want you to come with me." Keedie agreed and we sat and talked more about this new hustle.

I met with Cookie the next day, and he sold me a quarter brick. I didn't want to start off too big. Keedie wanted me to let him sell it around East Gate, so I gave him an eighth of a brick. He bagged it up and sold all of it in two days. Right away we noticed an amazing profit in cocaine. This was the start of a whole new ball game. I told Big Tone about what my plans were, but I never introduced him to Cookie. Without my connect, Big Tone had to come to me. It worked like a charm. Now all the family was selling cocaine for me, and I was the connect. We brought Sean on board, and things started moving even faster.

Keedie was still being hot headed and was starting to fuck with my nerves. Coming out of 7-Eleven one day, he saw this boy Ralph that owed him $200. They exchanged words, and I knew there was going to be a problem. "Where's my fuckin' money you owe me?" asked Keedie. Ralph started acting scared, and before I knew it, he started to run. Keedie pulled out a .44 handgun and shot four times at Ralph. Ralph fell to the ground screaming and crying. Later we find out Ralph had been shot in the ass.

"What the fuck did you do that for? Some punk-ass $200 debt?" I said.

"It's not about the fuckin' money, it's about the respect," Keedie replied.

"Let's see how much respect you get in jail, dumbass. This is the type of shit I don't need. You could have cut his ass off for the $200. Your case is going to cost much more than that," I said. Needless to say, I was mad as hell. I told him that he might have to get his own connect. I wasn't willing to put my whole operation in jeopardy for his silly-ass mistakes. We fell out real bad that day. I cut Keedie off for a while as far as business was concerned. I told him to handle the Ralph shit first. He sent his child's mom, Dana, to the hospital to pay Ralph off. He took the money because he was afraid.

Big Tone found out and told Keedie that he was a stupid dude for what he had done. Big Tone was also mad as shit. He called a meeting with us all. "Let me get to the point. All of y'all are young, and I know you're feeling a little big headed because of the money. Violence will bring all this shit to a quick stop. When detectives get involved, you're under investigation. We're hustlers not thugs. Thugs rob, shoot, and steal. Separate yourselves from any bullshit. Make money and stop fucking with your own livelihood. Stay low-key and stop being so flashy." After Big Tone finished what he had to say, he left the room. We had never seen him that mad. We sat quietly for a while and then we all made our contributions to the conversation. We had respect for one another. Only Big Tone was seen as a boss; we all saw one another as equal.

That night, we all went to the club to calm down and have fun. We all drank Remy Martin and messed with the girls. We could walk in any club and girls would point and stare at us. We thought we were the shit everywhere we went—always fresh in Gucci or Guess jeans or Abercrombie & Fitch, accompanied by big rope chains and nugget bracelets. I preferred Sergio Techini or Lacoste or Fila sweat suits, and I loved my big diamond pinky rings.

Keedie started getting into more and more trouble. One day out of the blue, Keedie called me; he was very upset and cursing at the top of his lungs. "I'm going to kill this muthafucka as soon as I see him! He's not going to keep putting his hands on my mother!" he said.

"Calm down and tell me what's up. Who the fuck are you talking about?" I asked.

"I'm talking about my mother's boyfriend Red. That muthafucka is putting his hands on my mother and I am not having that shit! I'm going over to her house to kill that muthafucka!" Keedie explained. He and Kenrick (his brother) decided to ride over to his mom's house immediately. It was in the projects, and everyone in the neighborhood knew them. Keedie didn't really give a damn who knew once he was mad.

They rolled up and entered their mom's house. Keedie walked in with a gun and headed to the back room looking for Red, he was coming out of the bathroom after having taken a shower. They exchanged words, and Red said that Keedie better kill him or Red would make one phone call and Keedie would be dead. "Muthafucka, don't you know that I kill for a living! That's my fuckin job! If you came to do work, then squeeze that shit!" Red screamed. The next sound heard was *bang, bang, bang, bang, bang, bang, bang, bang, bang*. Nine shots rang out and the gun was passed to Kenrick with a new clip. Nine more shots rang out right after that. The only other sound was Keedie and Kenrick's mom screaming.

"Wrap his ass up in the shower curtain and put him in the tub," Keedie said. They ran out and then drove off calmly.

Keedie called me that night and said we needed to meet up immediately, so we did, and he told me what had happened. Soon the word was all over the streets. We had started getting a rep in the street as real gangstas. Fear started to set in all over the neighborhoods. This was not what I had in mind. I just wanted to make money. Keedie had started making us hot all over. He liked the attention—good or bad. He always wanted to be known, and now everyone seemed to have heard about this shooting. Even the police knew about it and were starting to ask questions. Keedie and I lived in the same neighborhood in Maryland. He would always move around my way. If I moved, then he would move. Police watched him, so I knew they were looking at us all. Keedie started being more arrogant and crazy. He thought he was unstoppable. He turned me on to a new connect named L.A. who was a gambler with lots of money. He gambled in pool with Keedie's father who owned a pool hall. We hung out there all the time and became good with a billiard stick. Keedie's father introduced us to L.A. and told us not to fuck up his money. He never wanted to be in the middle. Whatever we paid for, L.A. would double in shipment. If we got twenty keys, he would give us forty bricks. We put our money together and went half on everything. Big Tone was so caught up with his girlfriend, Evonna, that he had no time for us. He was saying that we were getting out of control. Keedie started feeling heat about the Red murder but kept doing what he had to do.

One day, maybe three months later, this stuck-up kid name Blue was looking for Keedie. We figured it was over the Red killing. He came around the hood with some other boys in the car. We were contacted immediately about the matter. Two days later, I heard that Blue was killed in Central Gardens where he hung out. Keedie came to me and admitted the murder. He said Blue had to go. "That muthafucka was telling everyone he was going to kill me. I had to get at his ass. I'm not watching over my back, not for Blue or any of these muthafuckas!" Soon more talk was in the street. Now girls were calling us killers and saying that they wanted nothing to do with us.

One day, we were all in the house on Simms and things took a big turn. Big Tone was over; we hadn't seen him for weeks. Everywhere he went, he took Evonna with him. She didn't know that Big Tone had a warrant for his arrest in DC for parole violation. Big Tone went into the bathroom and stayed in there for a long time. I knocked on the door, and this muthafucka did the unthinkable. He opened the door and handed me a crack pipe that he was smoking. I was speechless and couldn't believe my eyes. "What the fuck are you doing? So now you're a damn crack head! All the fucking rules you gave us—and you're smoking crack!" I said.

"This is my god damn operation! You don't run me!" he screamed out in rage. "I put this shit together! I can handle my shit; you just handle yours!" I wanted to fuck him up, but it would have been a problem, so I just knocked the pipe out of his hand and left. I lost a lot of respect for Big Tone that day. We didn't talk much after that. Our relationship was strained to say the least. He called to say he was sorry and I was right. It never fixed things though. I looked at him as weak, and the respect level was lost.

A few months went by and I got a call that Big Tone was pulled over in DC and Evonna gave the police his real name, not knowing about the warrant. He was arrested and had to do his back up time. He called me for help on his rent, and that hurt me more to think he had smoked all his money up. This one girl had brought him to his knees. I paid his rent for a while, but we would argue because I refused to give Evonna money. "Why give a crack head money?" I would say. He was upset about me talking about his girlfriend. This was too much for me to deal with. I cut Big Tone off all together.

Meanwhile, Keedie was arrested for the murder of Red. Apparently the neighbors identified him as a possible shooter. He had no bond, so we just constantly visited him. Sean was already in jail for serving an undercover agent. He was a three-time felon and had no bond. Things were beginning to fall apart fast. We called my Jewish lawyer for Keedie, and months later he was given a bond. He put up his 560 SEC Benz to the lawyer. It was paid for, so it was collateral. Sean never got a bond and was sentenced to federal time.

Keedie getting out of jail didn't change his mind about anything. He was as wild as ever, and I think it affected me too. The police were asking about Blue's murder all the time. One day, I had just pulled up with cocaine to drop off and a .38 handgun. The vice jumped out on me and surrounded my vehicle. They were looking for the gun that killed Blue. Instead, I had three ounces of coke and a gun. The car was in my mother's name, so they called her. Because my lawyer showed that the drugs and gun were in a car not registered to me, they had to let me go. We were all without a leader now and very much out of control. All the attention and violence was bringing us down. This is what Big Tone had spoken against. Keedie had been fuckin' up his money, and I soon found out that he owed L.A. money. He was only paying with my money, and we were getting less cocaine. The police picked him up one morning and locked him up for Red's murder once again. They kept him for months with no bond, and then somehow on a technicality Keedie won his case.

Keedie was smoking PCP on a regular basis now and hanging with a new set of friends. I went on to my own friends and we talked periodically. He still had love for me, but we were on two different pages. L.A. wanted his money and wouldn't go away. Keedie called me one day out of the blue and wanted to meet up with me. He didn't sound like the friend I had always known; he sounded tired. "Hey, man, meet me at Steak in the Sack for some breakfast. I need to talk to you about some shit." We met up and he said he was going to meet up with L.A. to get some work. He wanted me to give him some of my money. He didn't realize that I knew about him owing L.A. money. He also didn't know I had moved on my own connect and was starting to distance myself.

"I'm not putting any money with you right now. Your ass is hot and I don't want to fuck with L.A. I saw L.A. in Georgetown and he didn't even speak to me. What the fuck is up with him?" I asked.

"I don't know what's up with him, but I'm going to find out," he said. He went out to meet L.A. the next day. Things didn't work out too well. Keedie met L.A. who was on the way to the airport with $250,000. He sent Keedie to meet up with a guy who was going to give them two bricks. Keedie met with the guy and got the bricks and then met L.A. at the airport. I was told he robbed L.A. for the $250,000. I knew this was going to be a problem. He didn't kill L.A., so we knew we would see him soon. Keedie laid low for weeks. Then one day, we were on our way to DC for some PCP exchange. Keedie had picked me up in a new Porsche 924S

Turbo. This He wanted to show off and we got up to about 130 mph. suddenly the car sped out of control. We went from one side to the other and then finally onto the embankment. I couldn't believe what had just happened. He looked at me and asked if I was all right. Then he calmly said, "Man, that was a hell of a Porsche commercial." That's when I knew he was gone out of his fuckin' mind. We got Wade the tow truck driver to pick us up, and then we rode on the flatbed to go get some PCP. After that day, I knew we had to part. The streets were talking, and L.A. was the talk. Everyone heard about the robbery because L.A. was everywhere with his goons. They were talking about killing Keedie's one-year-old, Kiki. Pops pleaded with L.A., but he was mad as hell at Keedie. L.A. had given us whatever we wanted, so he didn't understand why Keedie robbed him. Now I knew that the beef was going to be on. Keedie had finally crossed the line. L.A. and his gang were looking for Keedie all over the place.

Keedie came over to my house one night when it was raining. He was high as a kite. "Man, I want to talk to you for a moment. I know I might have fucked up, but I'm going to deal with it like a man. I don't want to put you in my shit anymore. I know you're a good dude, like my big brother. Just do me a favor and take care of little Kiki for me if anything goes bad," he said. "I'm going to Atlantic City for the week. I'll deal with this shit when I get back." We talked for a while, and then he left. I had a strange feeling come over me that day. He just didn't seem to be all right with himself. I think this time he knew he had crossed the line. L.A. was putting pressure on Keedie like never before. The street life was starting to leave a sour taste in my mouth. Things that I dreamed of having weren't so important anymore.

I wanted peace of mind, so I went to get my new friend Kim and then went back home. She always told me what was right and never sugarcoated anything. She wanted me to give up the game. "Stan, you're a great guy and you're wasting your life. You're too smart to be living this way. You can be anything you want to be. I'll help you. This is why I'm here. I don't care about your money. I love you for who you are," Kim said. Now I had never had a girl say these things to me. This was something new for me. She would sit and just wrap her arms around me in silence. Not a word would be spoken, but I heard everything she wasn't saying.

Kim and I had a great night and fell asleep. Early the next morning, I heard the phone ringing. I had a lot of girls, so I didn't want to answer in case it was one of them calling. Something told me that I needed to find my pager. I had left it in the car the night before. I went out to the car and found it in the seat. Immediately I saw 911111 all across the pager. It was Fats, the friend who had told me about Keedie owing L.A. money. I froze when I saw the number. I went back in the house to call back. "What's up, Fats? What's going on, man? Why are you 911-ing me?"

"Man I need to talk to you about some shit. I need you to sit down for this one."

In my mind, I already knew. "Man, fuck it," I said. "Just spit the shit, I'm ready for it." "Man ... I don't know how to say it, but man ... Keedie, man ... he umm, he umm ... is dead."

"Man, stop playing. I just talked to Keedie last night. Keedie's not dead. Who told you that dumb shit?"

"Stan, man, Keedie got killed in his car last night. He was speeding the rain on Pennsylvania Ave. and flipped the car over. He was thrown from the car and killed on the spot," Fats sadly revealed.

I was silent, and then my mind went blank as I dropped the phone to the floor. I couldn't bring myself to hang it up. I felt weak as though I was about to pass out. I sat on the bed with a blank face. Kima rushed to me as tears just rolled down my face with no expression. "What's wrong? What's wrong? Stan, please just talk to me. Please say something. Tell me what's going on." I must have just sat in silence for five minutes. I couldn't speak because of the lump in my throat. Tears ran down my face as I sat and stared at the wall. Time seemed to stand still, and a part of me died right at that moment.

Finally, I said, "Kima, Keedie's dead. He was killed in a car accident last night after we talked."

"Oh no!" she screamed, and then she hugged me and just cried. This was a sad time, and life as I knew it changed in that instant. Things seemed to have taken a turn for the worse—and fast.

"Is this what this shit is all about?" I said. "We're putting in all this work only to lose it all, including our lives? This is turning out to be some bullshit. I want more out of life than this, Kima. You're right; I can do better than this."

The days ahead seemed to get even worse. One thing I was thankful for was that somehow I thought Keedie gave his life in exchange for his daughter, Kiki. I knew she would live now. Somehow though, it never made me feel any better. I knew I had to tell my mother about this. She at one time loved Keedie and even kept Kiki. My aunt J who worked at the jail told my mother (actually she showed my mother) Keedie's record. That quickly changed her mind about him. She didn't like him around anymore after that. Mom was really tired of my lifestyle by now. She had never wanted that path for me and told me so all the time. Mom would even sometimes cry. She couldn't change my mind no matter how much she tried. She thought Kima was great and was glad to see us together. She would say Kima was good for me.

Mom was right and not just about Kima. She was also right about God. I knew in my heart, but I'm very stubborn. God had been talking to me for a very long time, but I always just kept running.

Keedie's family was not too business-like, so I knew I had to help. They didn't have money for his suit, so I got him a nice suit and made sure he looked nice. His brother Kenny called me to ask for my help. Days went by and it was finally time for the funeral. This was a hard day for me and my family. All of us had grown to love Keedie, and my friends were his friends. Kima was with me the whole time. She was being strong to keep me together. It was time for the funeral, and things just seemed to be getting harder for me to take. I pulled up in my Acura Coupe and saw cars and trucks everywhere. It was as though a movie star had died. Cars were all the way down and around the block. All of DC seemed to be there that day. Every drug dealer in the city came to pay respects to Keedie. Girls were crying, and men were crying just as hard. All kinds of people from lawyers to doctors were there. They all seemed to know Keedie. I had never seen so many walks of life, from thugs to businessmen, under one roof at the same time. People started walking over to embrace me and say they were sorry. They all knew me and knew our relationship was like brothers. The funeral started, and from start to finish, people never stopped crying. Even our lawyer, Mr. Baritz, was on hand. I walked up to the casket and talked to Keedie for a minute; I was swallowed with grief. We were all young, but Keedie was very young. I wished he could have only slowed down. As I stared at his body, a sudden calmness came over me. I heard a quiet voice come into my head. What I heard puzzled me at first, but then I quickly understood. "I did it my way," was all I heard.

Chapter 4
Becoming Heavy in the Game

I was turning into this monster that deep inside I really wasn't. People always told me that my personality didn't fit the profile of a dope boy. I wrestled with this lifestyle because I wanted the good things in life. By now, I was addicted to the lifestyle; it had become a part of me. I wasn't happy with myself, but somehow I just couldn't stop. It was like I was a ghetto superstar. Everyone knew my name, even when I didn't know theirs. I was a VIP everywhere we went. I was starting to feed into the status that people gave me. All the while, I was searching for peace I never could buy. Instead, I was buying cars every six months. More custom jewelry and clothes followed. Still I couldn't find the happiness that was supposed to come along with these things. I would get excited when things were new, but as soon as I was used to something, I would go out to buy more stuff. I stayed dressed in all the latest fashions.

In my mind, I heard my grandmother's voice pleading with me, trying to save my life. I often thought about her and all the things she had said to me. I really missed my grandmother. Mom was done with me and just wanted to distance herself. I had become a real embarrassment to her. She never raised me to be a gangster or a drug dealer. This was the path I chose, but I always thought that it somehow chose me. Mom told me that she was taking an overseas assignment in Germany. She wanted out, and deep inside it made me sad, but I definitely couldn't blame her. She and her husband, Chester, were leaving for Germany soon, and once again I felt like everyone I cared for was parting from my life. We gave Mom a party at a hotel just before she was due to leave. I have no brothers or sisters, so it was a very sad time for me. I felt like she was leaving my life for good. I guess I was about twenty-two years old at the time. Mom was also sad, but she tried to play it off so I wouldn't notice. She asked me if I wanted to move to Germany with her, but deep inside she knew that I wasn't going to do that.

The next day, she left for Germany (Heidelberg) and I had to face the reality of her being gone. I stayed to myself for some days and thought about what I wanted out of life. I was angry most of the time because I felt that all I had was myself. My new mentality was, *Stan, it's time for you to go hard.* It was all or nothing because I had no real family in Maryland. I had friends, but a lot of them were around for the money. I knew in my mind that if I was to fall, it would leave me pretty much homeless. I started taking life more seriously. I wanted to start a business of my own and make money legally. I had been beat out of my money already for trying to be legal, but it didn't change my mind. I was determined to make it work. I met this guy name Kool Aid from a hood called Langston Lane. He wanted a rim shop, and I saw an opportunity to do something legal. We hooked up and opened a rim shop in Maryland. I was his silent partner. The street game was still in effect, and I was still knee-deep in it. Kool Aid also sold drugs and had a great connect. He was very low-key, so we got along well. I was trying to stay low because of all the drama with Keedie. I was very popular in Maryland, and for the first time in my life, I didn't want to be. I wanted the money but not the fame.

Kima and I were getting closer and I was really starting to like her a lot. I still had other women, but not as many as I used to in the past. She was a good girl, so I tried to give her respect. Kool Aid was dating Kima's best friend, Tanya, so we hung out a lot. We started going to Atlantic City a lot more because Kool Aid loved to gamble. I was still working for the government (Harry Diamond Lab) and also had a rim shop. Mom wasn't calling me very often, so our relationship became strained. I think she was upset with me for who I had become.

Kima's family loved me, but they knew something was wrong. I had a BMW and a Cherokee Jeep and lots of money, and they knew it. What I didn't know was that her brother Derrick knew some guys that I knew and they had told him all about my drug dealing. He told his mom that he was scared for Kima because she wasn't that type of girl. One day I went over for dinner and they started asking me a lot of questions. I knew something had changed. Kima also knew something was wrong, but we didn't know what it was. I decided to cheer her up by taking her to a fur auction at a hotel in Go-Go Rockville. They used to send me flyers all the time, and this was a chance to see what it was all about. We went and they had all types of fur coats from short to full length. I started bidding and ended up getting a coat for Kima for $1,400. The coat was worth about $3,500. She was happy, but Kima wasn't the type of girl you had to buy things for. She was just happy with love. I decided that she should move into my apartment with me. She was a little older than me, so she was ready to settle down. Kima really wanted me to stop selling drugs and just work. She begged me to quit, but I was young and didn't want to quit until I had first established a strong legal foundation. I knew that money was an addiction, so I needed to be able to replace it with something. She moved in and things were good for a while.

One day, I was taking out the trash and I noticed four agents in a car wearing blue jackets with yellow writing. I played it off like I didn't see them and continued to the trashcan. I noticed a van that also looked strange in the parking lot. I went in the house and told Kima to quickly pack up and go to her mom's house. "Hurry up and grab some clothes and go. I'll tell you about it later, but you have to go now," I said.

She got hysterical and started crying. "I won't leave you if something's wrong. I love you and we're in this together. Tell me what's wrong," she said.

"I can't talk about it now—go quickly. I'll call you and tell you about it tomorrow. Here's my lawyer's number and here's $50,000 in cash. Take this and don't look around, just walk to your car and go." After Kima left, I began cleaning up what drugs I had. Then I climbed off my patio and started running. When I got away from the apartment, I called someone to come pick me up. After all that, the next day I learned that they were raiding the apartment next to my building. It made me realize that this was no life for Kima to be involved in. I talked to her the next day, and I wasn't happy about what I had to say but knew it was necessary. "Kima, last night the police raided a house in the next building. I thought when I took out the trash that they were coming for me, so I made you leave. This is no life for you to be involved in. I love you too much to get you killed or arrested. You should move home with your mom. I'm caught up in this lifestyle now and this is what I'm married to. You wouldn't understand, but it's for the best." Kima didn't say a word but just broke down crying. I knew she understood, but it still hurt. She began once again to beg me to quit the lifestyle.

"Baby, please stop this life for me. I'll work two jobs if that's what it takes. We can make it without this drug life. It's not worth it to give up your life in jail or be killed. You have money and a job now. We can make it if we just work together. Please don't do this to us," she pleaded. Every word Kima spoke fell on deaf ears at the time. I didn't want to hear shit about getting out of the game. In my mind, I was married to the street and it was till death do us part. The crazy part about this was that I knew she was right. She said all the right things to convince me to stop. It even made sense, but I was totally addicted to the lifestyle.

I came to find out that my neighbor, who I never knew sold drugs, had ten bricks of cocaine and fifty pounds of weed in his apartment. He was an older guy, and we never suspected him. They showed the raid on the news and that's how I knew. Kima packed up and left me the next day after our talk. She was very hurt because she wanted to get married. I was lost in my own world and didn't even know it. We started to drift apart because she couldn't take the lifestyle anymore. I respected her decision and we remained friends. Many other women were still on me at that time, so it was easy for me to adjust—though I knew that the women I started seeing didn't care about me, just the money. They never wanted me to stop. I had every kind of car from an Acura Coupe to trucks. They liked the fact that they could ride in style and be seen with a D-boy. I was becoming numb to this shit, and the death of Keedie made me worse. The pain of losing my best friend made me less patient and more violent. I was always looking for a way out, but it seemed useless. Everyone was selling or using drugs in DC and Maryland. It didn't seem so bad at the time because everyone was doing it.

I met this girl name Angel, and she was bad. She was known in the streets, but it never bothered me. She was sexy and very stylish. She was fuckin' with this old dude from uptown named Fred. He was a big-time heroine dealer, and everyone knew him. When we went out, we would always sneak to places out of city limits. We went to Baltimore a lot. I would take women down to Baltimore because they had good seafood and I wasn't well known there. Angel was too hot, so it didn't last long. I had so many different women at that time my neighbors would see me and just shake their heads. I had a different girl every day. I was single, so in my mind it was okay. I met a girl named Cinnamon. She was freaky and fun. She knew how to have a good time. She loved to laugh and just wild out. She was down for whatever, so I quickly put her to work. She started holding bricks for me. I would cook up at her house, and she would do the bagging while I did the cooking. She was fine as shit and had an ass that would shame J-Lo. All she wanted to do was fuck and have fun. Her dude was locked up for murder, so he was going to be out of the picture for a while. Needless to say, she caught me out with her girlfriend one day, so that was the end of that. She still wanted to see me, but I played by the rules. Once you get caught, leave her, because she'll always be on get back.

Kima, my old girl, still came around from time to time, but she knew I had too many other women so she never fully wanted to get back with me. One day, Kool Aid called and started asking me all this shit about Kima. "Man, you fucked my shit up with my girl. Now she's hanging out trying to comfort your girl, and I can't get any pussy. You need to get back with her ass. What did you do to that girl, man?"

"Man, Kima's a great girl and I just don't want to fuck her over. You know she's trying to get married and shit. I can't do that right now," I explained. "Fuck all that. What's up with you, man?"

"Come see me, that's what's up with it," said Kool Aid. So I went over to see him and he had enough bricks to build a house. The numbers were good, so here I go again. Kool Aid was a bamma-ass dude. You would never think he hustled. This nigga would wear anything—and I mean anything. He was from SE (Langston Lane). He started getting jealous of me because he knew I was moving things fast, which meant I was getting money. He had this brother from Cali that moved with him. I never trusted his ass. Kool Aid had a bad gambling habit and so he started fuckin' up his money. One day, I was at the movie with this chick and when I got home my house had been broken into. Kool Aid had sent his brother to rob me. I knew it was his ass. I was mad as shit, but I had to keep calm. I went to the rim shop the next day, and my silver dollar pieces were in a jug in his office. He thought I wouldn't notice. I played it off. I called up a few of my head busters and told them what was up. Even though it killed me, I played it off like I didn't know. I called Kool Aid about a week later to see if he had work. "Come see me," he said, which meant yes. Now his work was going to be my work. I told my youngins what to do, and you know how the story went. Let's just say I came up. About a year later, he was killed in a drug transaction gone badly. This was the way it was in DC. You had to stay on your game or be killed. Everybody is quick to shoot in DC. They'll kill you in a heartbeat.

    After I came off, I chilled for a few months to think. I would stop from time to time just to cool off. Now I had this homeboy named Skinny who was down. He was doing okay, but I knew I could make it better. I started dumping on him. He got me paid and became real cool with me. We started hanging out a little. My freak girl Cinnamon was cool with his girl. All of us hung out a lot and ate at different restaurants. We sometimes went to basketball games or whatever. In my mind, things were starting to take a turn for me. I wasn't feeling this drug dealer thing anymore. All my friends were dying and life was starting to take a toll on me. I had been to so many funerals that I was numb to it. Dying had become a reality for me. I was almost starting to expect death. I didn't have many of the friends that I had before because many had been killed. Others were in jail doing big numbers. I started hearing my grandmother's words in my mind more and more. My mother's words would also ring out loudly from time to time. Mom was gone and things just weren't the same. I felt alone, and this really bothered me a lot. I felt that I had no one I could trust. With no brothers or sisters, you grow up learning that all you have is you. I think that has a lot to do with the women companions. They kept me from being alone.

Now, Skinny used to want to switch cars a lot. He had this 300 Z Turbo that was hot, so I would switch sometimes. One day, I switched with him and met this girl while at a red light. She was on the bus, and I was talking to her through the window. I convinced her to get off at the next stop. She got in and we began to talk. She told me her name was Tawana, and we went and sat at Popeye's to grab something quick. "How spontaneous are you?" I asked.

"Very," she answered.

"Okay, then let me take you on a weekend trip right now."

"Where are you trying to take me?" she asked.

"To Kings Dominion."

"Stop playing, you are not taking me to Kings Dominion."

"Yes I will, if you want to go," I said.

"Okay, then let me go and get my clothes." So we did that and then went to my house so I could get some clothes and lock down my house. We took off for Kings Dominion and had a ball. She was fun and crazy, so it was all good. She made me laugh and the sex was great. We stayed in the park all day and funned out. For the moment, she took all my problems away. Then Skinny called looking for me.

"Hey, mothafucka, where are you?"

"Man, I'm at Kings Dominion with this bad-ass chick."

"What the fuck are you doing down at Kings Dominion?" he asked. He knew that I was wild, so it was no telling.

"Man, it's a long story, but you're going to laugh your ass off when I tell you," I said laughing.

"Well guess where I am, nigga? I'm in Atlantic City with this bitch I met at the mall," he said.

"I'm on my way back now because my phone has been blowing up," I said. "I'm sitting on a lot of work, so get your rest because when you get back it's time to go to work." I said. Plus my numbers went down.

"Shit I'll leave now if that's what it is," said Skinny.

"Nah, you're good. Enjoy yourself and call me when you hit the city," I said.

"Aye, man, make sure you hit me first before anymore of your youngins get word. I know how fast you be getting rid of them things," said Skinny. This was my man, so I always looked out for him. He was a good dude and made me lots of money. My Eastern Ave crew also was getting me paid. I didn't want people to get suspicious about all this work I had, so I moved it only with my main runners. They were happy because my numbers had become cheaper. Fats, my youngin from Eastern Avenue, ran the block for me. My main strips had become Glenarden, Village in the Woods, Fairfax Village, and Eastern Avenue. Those were some hoods that could do a brick or half a brick a day on any strip. This was great for me, but I still had a different look on it all. Fats was cool, but he didn't have a lot of heart, so he was my weak link. He was the one I watched the most. I knew he wouldn't be able to hold up, so I didn't tell him much.

I was doing well as far as money goes, but I needed a way out. I wanted to be a businessman, not a drug dealer. I was looking for a way out. The streets were what I knew, but I was determined to learn a new hustle. My uncle said that a real hustler knows more than one hustle. I knew if I could run a street business at this level, then I could run a legitimate company. I started a T-shirt company called Undaground Sportswear. I was selling shirts out my truck, in stores locally, and however I could. My shirts started to do well, and soon I was looking for a retail space. I was starting to feel like I was worth something. Drug dealing just didn't make me happy. I knew I was smarter than that deep down inside. I felt loved but hated all at the same time.

We all loved to go to the local fights. DC is known for boxing. One day, about thirty of us went to a fight at the Convention Center. I saw a girl there that didn't look familiar. I went over and talked to her, and she was very down to earth. She said her name was Tanny. This was after I said my name was Stan. I thought she was trying to be smart. "No, my real name is Tanya," she stated. So we hit it off well and went to IHOP after the fight was over. I was supposed to call her the next day for a movie date. Well I didn't, and she called me the next day. "Thanks for standing me up yesterday," she said.

"I'm sorry but I got tied up."

"Too tied up to call? That's rude, but you won't get that chance again. You must be used to girls sweating you, but that's not me," she said angrily.

"I'm sorry, you're right. Let me make it up to you," I said.

"Don't do me any favors. I don't get stood up by any man and then date him a second time," she said.

I said, "Good, this will be your first time. I'm not taking no for an answer. As a matter of fact, I'm on my way to your house," I said jokingly. She started laughing and said that she had never seen anyone as confident as me before. I knew this was going to be my girl. So she gave me her address and I headed that way. I didn't know it at the time, but she was very street smart. I thought she was slow because she lived in Virginia. Most Virginia girls are green or not street smart. This was not the case at all. She had been living in Inglewood, California, so she was familiar with getting money and guys who were getting money. I picked her up and told her we would get some breakfast. I picked her up in an old Subaru. What I liked was that she never mentioned the car. We had a good conversation over breakfast, and then I asked her to go to the car lot with me. I picked out a 300 CE Coupe. I tried to impress her, but she didn't blink. So what do you think about my car?" I said.

"It's a car. I'm used to cars, Stan, so you don't have to try to impress me."

I wasn't used to this type of chick. I said, "Damn, you could at least be happy for me. I'm used to cars too, but—shit—this one is hot," I said.

"I love your car, don't get me wrong, but the Subaru was working fine," she said in a sexy voice. I proceeded to purchase the car after our test drive. I called one of my youngins and told him to come pick up my Subaru for me. We left in the Benz. She told me while driving that she needed to tell me something. I was thinking, *Oh shit, now what is she going to say*? "Stan, when I was in Cali, I met this guy in Foot Locker who told me to pick out anything in the store and he would buy it. He then called his boss and said, 'This girl is so bad, you have to meet her.' So I got on the phone and he said he wanted to hookup. Long story short, I was given a job of counting his money every Saturday with a money counter. No you see why money is not that important to me?"

"Yeah, damn, I see what you mean."

"So let me just get to know you for you," she said with a smile. That's how she got my ass. Now we started hanging out more and more. I was really getting into Tanny. Alexander O'Neil came to DC, and she bought my ticket. I wasn't used to women doing that for me. I always paid. So after the show, we went to my place and had sex. I was so nervous about this girl that I was a two-minute man. We both laughed, but she was mad for real. Now I knew I was going to have to make it up to her. She took my car and went home to get some things to spend the night. She came back and cooked a meal for me, and I knew I was hooked after that.

"You can cook your ass off. I didn't think you knew shit about pots and pans," I said jokingly.

"I knew you thought that, so I wanted to cook for you so you could see for yourself." So that night I gave her some of the best sex I had. I even gave her my signature move. She was hooked after that.

Skinny and Fats were blowing up my phone now. "Man, what the fuck you been doing for two days?" said Skinny. "Maybe you got money, but we still hungry over here. You all pussy-whipped and shit," he said. Girls were also blowing my phone up, but I was really getting into Tanny.

Meanwhile, Mom was on her way back to the States. I was really thinking about getting out of the game. The problem became my workers. What would they do without me fronting them work? How were they going to eat? I decided I was going to call a meeting. I called my main men and told them to meet me at Houston's in Georgetown. We met and I told them that I wanted to have a serious talk.

"All right, nigga, what the fuck is this all about? Let me guess, your ass is getting married or some shit," said Skinny.

"Hell no, mothafucka, I'm not getting married. This is a business meeting, dumbass. Look y'all, here's the deal. I got my cash up, now I want to get legal. I bought a store, and now I want to just to get out of the street. This is what I came to talk about."

"So what the fuck are we suppose to do while you're straight? We suppose to get a job?" said Fats, pissed off.

"Slow down, nigga, let me finish. I need all y'all to start stacking paper and working on your plan. I told y'all asses to have a plan B. Now you see why I said that shit when Keedie died. So now I want to do real business. I'm giving everyone six months to get your shit together. If you come up with something, I'll help back it. I'm trying to be fair to all of y'all. I respect all of y'all like brothers. Otherwise I wouldn't have called the meeting. I'm good enough to walk and say fuck it, but that wouldn't be right. Now if you want to stay in the game, then I'll turn you on to another homeboy. He's not going to have my numbers, but he'll let you eat. I'm starting to feel hot now because a lot has happened around me. I just got offered a storefront and I need to focus on something legal. If I go to jail, y'all asses would starve anyway, so consider this shit a look out."

B, my new soldier from Edgewood, was mad because I had just put him on. "Damn, man, so you know where that shit is going to leave me. I respect you, but, man, that's some sellout-ass shit. You put me on and off all at the same time. I got my son to feed, so what now for me?" he said. While B was talking, he got loud because of his anger. My other crew didn't know B was like that, because he was new. They looked at me like; *do you need us to fuck him up?* I think he caught the hint and quickly calmed his ass down.

"Look, B, you're a good dude, but I just want you to know that you better stay in your fuckin' lane with this conversation. I let you get down with us, so respect that shit, mothafucka. Now do you have a problem with that?" I asked.

"My bad man, you right."

I started to not trust him after the meeting, so his work became less and less. Plus I didn't like how he came at me. Anyway, we all ate and drank that night and started talking over a plan or two. After we ate, we all went to the strip club. The strippers loved us because we had that white and money. We never paid for dances because they'd rather have the powder. I must say life was fun at this time. My crew seemed to have more respect for me than ever. It was like they realized at the time just how important I was to them.

Meanwhile, Tanny and I were going strong. We started taking trips a lot, and she showed me how to enjoy life more. I finally told her I was opening a beauty and barber supply store. She was very happy for me. The next day, I took her and showed her. We ended up having sex in the vacant space. Okay, I'm going to keep it real. I had sex with every girl I brought to the store. I was still a playboy, but not as much. Soon, I started noticing shit about Tanny that I didn't like. Christmas came, and I bought her a nice pair of studs and a tennis bracelet. She told me she didn't like the bracelet because the diamonds were cloudy. I started thinking she was crazy. My next move was to show her ass a thing or two. I took it back and told her I was buying another one. When I took it back, I got my mom something with the money. This was the beginning of the end. I went out of town for New Year's on business and left Tanny my Benz. She decided to let her boss drive my car and it got back to me. Now true, I was selling it, so her reason was that he wanted to buy my car. "Tell me why you're late picking me up from the airport and my car is on empty?" I asked, mad as shit. She didn't say anything. The gold digger in her started to show, and I realized it was always there from the start. So back to my player ways. I was starting to think all girls were fuckin' gold diggers.

Redds was a girl I kept in the cut. She didn't ask for much; she just wanted to snort powder a lot. We always had fun together when we hung out. I called her and said, "Let's go to Florida for four days. I'll pay for the trip, just pack your shit." She had a cool boss, so it was all good. We made the trip for two weeks later and were out. Now Redds was a Redbone with hazel eyes and the fattest ass in the world. She was a real sweetheart from Maryland. I knew her from high school, and I knew her brother also. They were from a good family. Redds would invite me over and cook and then fuck me all night. She had some fly-ass girlfriends too. As a matter of fact, Big Tone's girl, Evonna the crack head, used to be with Redds. When I came home, Tanny said she was coming over to see me. I knew something was wrong. She came over and started back to my room. When she came out of the closet, she was holding Redds's tag from my luggage. "What the fuck is this, Stan? I thought you were in Florida with your boys," she said while crying. "You're a lying piece of shit. I knew you were cheating on me. You're just like the rest of these DC niggas," she said. Then she tried to fight me and picked up my phone and threw it out the door.

"Hold up, Tanny, you're going too far. Matter of fact, your ass has to go." So I called her Aunt Becky who she lived with at the time. "Becky, I want Tanny out my house because she's going to make me put my hands on her. I'm not trying to do that, but she's in my house trippin." "Let me speak to Tanny for a minute, Stan, if you don't mind."

"Tanny, get the phone, it's your aunt."

"What the fuck you call her for? I'm not leaving this fucking house until you explain this shit!" she screamed at the top of her damn lungs.

"Becky, she won't come to the phone, so I'm going to call you back," I said.

"Stan, please don't hurt my niece. I know you have a temper, but try to remain calm because I know Tanny. Could you do that for me?" she begged.

"Yeah, Becky I got you. I'm not going to put my hands on her." As soon as I got off the phone she tried to steal me in my face. I quickly grabbed her hands and put her in a chair. "Come on, Tanny, you know what I do, so why don't you chill?"

"I don't give a fuck what you do, Stan. You're wrong," she said, crying.

"Look, Tanny, I'm sorry for what I did. You're right; I'm wrong for this. So let me ask you something, do you want to stay with me or do you feel this is over?"

"Stan, you know I don't want to leave. I'm hurt, but I love you, so I'm staying. I want you to do me right and treat me like I deserve to be treated. I'm not a hoe or freak. I'm a lady, Stan. I have your back no matter what. How could you do this to us? You told me you loved me." She was still crying.

"Tanny, look, I fucked up and I'll do right by you. You know this is different though. You know how these girls be trying to get at me. Even your cousin Tee tried to fuck me. You know I keep shit real with you. So let's stop this shit right now."

"Well call that bitch and cancel her shit now while I'm standing here. Show me that you fuck with me. Or do you need me to do it?"

"Tanny, this not a fucking relationship I got with this girl. We just took a trip together, but we not into nothing."

"So this bitch is just your hoe, huh? You just call her when it's time to fuck. That's some nasty shit. How many other bitches are you fuckin', Stan?"

"Tanny, how many niggas are you fucking? Don't let me get on your shit. I know half of DC and Maryland, and the streets are talking. That bitch-ass nigga Rico from NW is saying your name. They said you were in his 850 BMW outside Houston's talking. If I would have walked up on your ass, I would have flipped that motherfucking car over with that choppa," I said angrily.

"See, that's your problem; you listen to your hating-ass friends. All of them just want to fuck me, so they mad. I wasn't never in Rico's car. If I wanted Rico, I would be with him, but I love Stan and he don't even know it. That's what your problem is."

"Fuck this shit, Tanny. I got some business to handle, so go home and we'll talk."

"I'm not leaving this house tonight. I want to spend the night."

"All right, well I'll be back. I'll call you in a little while," I said.

Wow, this quickly became a pattern for us as time went on. We would be good this week, but next week would be hell. I had an apartment out by Tanny's house. This girl Tiny worked in the clubhouse there. She was bad with an ass that was so fat it looked fake. I didn't know at the time that she knew Tanny. I hollered at her one day while dropping off the rent. Next thing I know she invited me over. This girl was so cool, and I liked to hang out with her. Needless to say, the sex was great. For some reason, she liked me to hit her in the rear. I'm not into that, but I took care of that for her. She would just put it there on her own. One day she sent flowers to my store with her panties, some Remy Martin, sunflower seeds, and a condom all in a basket. I thought that shit was sexy. She called me and asked to see me for lunch. "Can I come to the store and see you?" she asked.

"Sure, bring your good pussy ass up here. I want to see you anyway. Bring me something good to eat."

"Okay, I'm on my way." When she got to my store, we ate and then fucked in my office. Then Tanny found out about the basket and went off crazy. Tiny set that shit up to break us up. She had help from Tanny because the girl Tisa who worked for me at the store told Tanny about the basket and who Tiny was, so Tanny went on Tiny's job and confronted her. Tiny got scared and told it. Now I was in trouble again. This happened over and over until things started getting too bad. We ended up breaking up over this one.

Two weeks went by and my man Fats called me. "Stan, I need to rap to you about something."

"What's up? Is it business?" I asked.

"No, it's about Tanny. Are you still seeing her or what?"

"No, I'm not with her anymore. Why? What's up, nigga?"

"Well Daryl called and said she was fucking Blackhole from 58th. They were at the bowling alley together last night. They went out of town too," he said.

"Okay, that's cool; we're not together, so she can fuck who she wants to. I'm fucking, so you know what it is at the end of the day, I'm on my G shit," I said laughing.

As soon as his ass hung up the phone, I called that hoe. "What's up with you? Are you near my house?"

"No I'm not, but I could be," she said. "Why do you miss me?"

"Yeah I do, so why don't you come over. I'll be home around ten o'clock."

"Okay, I'll be over. Just let me know when you get home and I'll be on my way," she said.

Now I was mad as shit, but I had to play it off. If she knew I knew, then she wouldn't come. Tanny pulled up in front of the apartment and I instantly lost it. I tried to wait until we got into the house, but my anger wouldn't let me. "Tanny, what's up with you and that mothafucka Hole? My man said you were fucking him. Bitch, we just broke up two weeks ago. How are you taking dick that fast if you cared about me?" I asked with my hand around her neck.

"Wait, Stan, let my neck go please. I didn't fuck him. We're just friends and we went out a few times—that's all. I swear I didn't fuck him!"

"Oh so his own brother Daryle would lie on him. You didn't know that I knew Daryle. See, bitch, you're always lying to me!"

As we went back and forth, the police pulled up. I got myself together as the officer asked me if everything was all right. I had a 9mm pistol on me as he was talking to me. He explained that someone had called about a disturbance. He then asked Tanny if she was okay. The look on his face said, *please let her say no so I can cuff this nigga*. I was surprised when she said she was fine. The officer asked us to keep it down and then pulled off.

"Tanny, you know what, I knew you had that in you from the start, but I was pussy-whipped. But since I'm not now, you can leave and I won't be calling you anymore."

Tanny still had her house, so I needed to get my money. I called her later that night to say I was coming to get my money. She got quiet all of a sudden. "Can you come later because I was going to get Tee and hang out?"

"No, I'm on my way now. I need to get my money so you can move on," I said.

"Stan, are you sure this is what you want? I mean, I love you and I think we can work it out. You did me wrong and I did you wrong, but I think we should try to work it out," she pleaded.

"Nah, I'm not feeling that. I just want my money so you can move on. I don't trust you anymore because you're on money too hard."

"Then fuck it. Just come get your money. Whatever."

For some reason, I knew there was going to be some bullshit in the game. I arrived about fifteen minutes later, and she was in the back room. I went straight to the basement where she stayed and opened my safe to empty it. I started counting the money. It was supposed to be twenty-five thousand, but there was only eighteen thousand. "Tan, you need to get down here. I need to rap to you about something."

"What's up, Stan? What do you need to talk about now?" she asked.

"About my mothafuckin money—that's what. Why is this shit short and where's the rest of my shit?" I asked.

"Stan, I don't have your money because I don't go in your safe. You never gave me the combo to the safe anyway."

"You're a damn liar because let me remind your ass about the crazy shit you did. Remember when I had Skinny's Z and you got mad and called the police on me and told them that I had a gun on me? Well that's the day I gave you the combo to get money for my bond. I didn't know at the time that you were the one that called the fuckin' police in the first place. I should have left your ass then. If you lied to me then, of course you'll steal from me. This shit is a wrap." I stood up with my bag of money and started taking shit off her dresser for the money she stole. I took a Gucci watch, the diamond studs, and a chain I bought.

"Give me my shit, Stan. I'm not playing," she said while screaming for Beck."

"Tanny, fuck you, you some trash. You don't have to worry about me again, trust me."   "Good," was her response. After that, I never said much to Tanny again. I wanted to tell my bouncer girl to punch her in the face, but I gave her a pass. She was right about what she said; at the end of the day, we both had done some bullshit to each other. No one could blame anyone because when we first met, she was all on me and I dropped the ball. So I can own that now.

Tiny was still in the ring, but she was starting to be a bugaboo or a pain in the ass. She knew I had stopped dealing with Tanny, so now she thought she could move in. She was talking about moving to Atlanta, so I was thinking that would be good for me and her. She was a real good girl, but much too needy.

I was back to thinking about quitting the game and retiring from it all together. I had told my crew already, and now things were getting really old.

Chapter 5
The Death of Skinny

My relationship with my mother was definitely not the same anymore. She was only concerned with her and her husband at the time. When she was in Germany, I never heard from her, so this was part of the reason. She didn't know me anymore. I had become a man, and she still thought I was a little boy. We would talk, but it just wasn't the same.

Skinny called me about some work. He said he was done, so I knew what he wanted. He was starting to get money big time around Fairfax Village. He was doing it out of the house, which I was against. I took about a half a brick to his house around ten o'clock that night. "What's up, Skinny? What are y'all niggas doing up in here?" I asked joking.

"Nigga, waiting on your slow ass to get here. I already missed about five thousand waiting for you. I know you was somewhere with a bitch," he said laughing.

"No, not this time I wasn't. I had to wait for my man to bring it to me. He didn't have a half, so he had to break it down for me. You know I'm trying not to touch this shit. The feds would love to have me before you losers," I laughed. "Why are you answering the door with no gun? Oh I see, it's in the chair. So what—you keeping the chair safe?" I asked.

"Nah, but I'm good. My brother put it over there. I got this shit, man. These dudes know what time it is around here!" Skinny said with a serious face.

"Yeah okay, they know. Man, don't you know that it's no honor amongst thieves. Keep that damn Glock on your hip and be smart. Never underestimate any man," I said.

"Nigga, there you go preaching again. I ain't trying to hear all that shit, nigga. Where's my shit?"

I then reached in my pants and pulled out a half brick of powder and then left around eleven o'clock or so. It felt funny that night; something just didn't sit right with me, but I couldn't put my finger on it at the time. Later that night, I got a phone call at around 2 a.m. This shit always made me nervous. It was usually bad news and I had heard enough of that for ten people. It was Skinny's brother, LoLo. He was yelling and upset. "Nigga, they shot my brother! These mothafuckas shot Skinny! I don't believe my brother's dead, man! They shot my brother, Stan. Man, this shit is fucked up."

For a while, I was totally numb and couldn't move. I was speechless because I had just left him. "Calm down and tell me where you're at right now," I finally said.

"I'm at home, and his body is lying in the floor in a pool of blood. They robbed him and stabbed him during a fight. Then they shot him!"

"I don't believe this shit. Man, sit tight. I'll be there in ten minutes!" It normally took maybe twenty minutes, but not tonight. I grabbed my 9mm and headed out the door. When I got there, his other brother, who was a policeman, was there. He told me what was going on and we talked. I still didn't believe it was happening. They said Skinny's girlfriend was on the phone with him and heard everything. She told them who it was, and that's all I wanted to hear at that time. Tears fell from my eyes, but I was too mad to wipe them dry. I could only think about how good of a guy my homeboy was. He never deserved this. He was a great kid and wasn't into anything but trying to eat. His mom had quit her job and was depending on him to support her.

I had planned a trip and paid for it, but now I wasn't going to make the trip because of the funeral. It was going to be hard for me to see him in a casket after we had just seen each other laughing. Skinny was a happy guy who always had jokes. It was a hard decision for me, whether to go to the funeral or remember our last day. I chose to do the latter. I wanted to see him the way I had already remembered him. I went on the trip and missed his funeral. To some it was wrong, but I couldn't handle seeing my little man in a casket. I had been down that road too many times. Needless to say, the trip was a waste. I couldn't enjoy the girl or the trip because my mind was on murder. I knew this one couldn't slide. I was ready to get home to make it happen. Days went by, and the trip was finally over.

I came home and had a small meeting. I called on a few of my goons and LoLo to come so he could show us who and where. LoLo was afraid to get involved, so we had a problem. "Man, you won't tell me who these mothafuckas are so we can take care of business? What kind of shit is that? These mothafuckas shot Skinny, and you don't want to handle it? Are you serious, nigga?"

"Man, if I do something to get locked up, then my mother would die from that shit. She already begged me and I made her a promise not to do anything!"

"LoLo, man, you don't have to do anything but show me where these niggas are at. You don't have to be involved with this. My little man and his crew will do the rest." He agreed, so we came back two days later with guns in hand and a stolen car. "Okay, LoLo, we just need you to show us who it is, okay?"

"I can't do it, Stan, because I don't want to hurt my mother." My man got so mad at LoLo for being a bitch, he wanted to shoot him. I was just as mad too.

"Man, nigga, this is some crazy shit you telling me. They killed your brother, nigga. Did you hear what I just told you, man?" LoLo started crying and never said another word. We couldn't believe the shit. I got mad and started cursing at LoLo. It didn't work though. He just sat and looked out the car window. We slowly pulled off and took him to his car. I lost my respect for LoLo after that. We never talked much after that day.

When I got home that night, I was by myself, so I had time to think. I needed to focus on my store and getting my shit in order. Maybe God saved me for a reason, I started thinking. All my friends were dying but me. Maybe it was God that didn't let us kill those bastards. Maybe God had another plan for my life. This started to take root in my mind. All the things my mother and grandmother had once told me were ringing in my thoughts. I started getting more focused, and then I made up my mind to leave the game for good. I just wanted a clean start on life. I was going to make the beauty and barber supply store work out.

Mr. Gille owned a barber school, and I was a student. He offered me the space next door. I took him up on it and decided to open a beauty and barber supply store. The school was next door, so I figured this would be a good opportunity to sell clippers to the students. He gave me time to build out the space for free. He was a fair man. He was also rich, so he didn't really care what I did. I put lots of time into it because it was my way out. I knew that you get out of something what you put into it. I had cash, so I paid for all of my supplies, shelving, etc. out of pocket. The word quickly spread about me leaving the game, and some people were glad and some were mad. I knew that it wouldn't be easy, but it was something I felt I had to do for myself. A lot of people tried to help me, so this made it easier for me to open sooner than I thought I thought I'd be able to. Most of the girls were happy for me and wanted to help. Redds helped me with the programming of the cash register because I had never run one in my life. She showed me how to work it and reprogram it in case something went wrong. For some reason, when you own a business, more women of all walks of life become interested in you. Maybe the legal business was attractive to them. It damn sure wasn't the money I was used to getting.

    I knew that it wouldn't be possible with one store. I got with some of the top hairstylist in DC and Maryland to find out about the products they used. It helped a lot, so I didn't have products just sitting. I was a barber, so I wanted to cater to the barbers, which was opposite of most beauty and barber supply stores. This would prove to be my niche. I bought a van so that my supplies could be delivered. I was finally proud of what I was accomplishing. The store was only about a thousand square feet and had been a carpet business before I took over. I had Ray come in and redo the whole store. It turned out really nice. The building was old, but other than that, it was in great shape. It was around June or July, and it was hot as hell in the store because there was no air in the building. Mr. Gille was going to install it, but it had not happened yet. Meanwhile, I had already started to let people buy things just to see how much traffic it would generate. About a month later, I decided to have my grand opening, and it was a big day. People came from all over the city to show support. This was a good sign. I felt that the store was going to be a life changer for me. It would give me some real responsibility.

    Big Mike was the guy who ran Mr. Gille's school next door. Big Mike and I were cool, so he always looked out for me. Mr. Gille had agreed not to sell clippers to the students anymore once I opened, but he didn't keep his word. However, I became so known to the students for making deals that they still came to my store. Now because I was a barber, I set up a station in back of the store. I was a one-man shop, but it was fly. I would cut by appointment only, mostly my homeboys or associates. Things were starting to feel right for once. Tanny still showed me love and sent flowers to say congrats. I thought that was cool. Not everyone was happy about the store. Some people were haters because I was doing legal business, and they felt stuck in the game. People would ask if I could make moves for them still, but I wouldn't do it anymore. I really wanted a new and better life for myself.

 A few months went by and I was out to breakfast with Tanny. We hadn't seen each other in a while, so she wanted to meet. While we were eating, I got a call from my younger cousin from New York. "Hey, nigga, these dudes are at Aunt J's house with guns after Cam." Cam was another crazy-ass little cousin. "They say he owes them money for some weed, and they trippin," Anthony explained.

 "Damn, man, I can't even eat my food in peace without some dumb shit going on. Y'all fake-ass gangsters don't have a gun?"

 "Nah, man, you know I'm just visiting, and Cam said they don't have no strap."

 "Okay, look I'll be up there in fifteen minutes. Just let me eat first." I was thinking; *don't even go over there*, but if one of them got hurt, it would be on me now.

 Tanny said to me, "Please don't go over there, Stan. You're doing good now, so don't let them set you back."

 "Yeah, you're right, but I can't leave those little niggas hanging. I'm just going to make sure everything is cool. I'm not going to do anything crazy."

 "Well do you have a gun on you?"

"Come on, Tanny, you know damn well I got a gun on me. When have you known me not to have a gun?"

So we got there, and the police pulled up around the same time. I got out of the car, walked over to my aunt, and asked what was going on. Before she could answer me, some bitch-ass nigga asked me what the fuck was I supposed to be doing about the situation. The police were removing him while he yelled this out. I laughed and told him that I would see how he felt when the police left. "Let them do their job, tough guy. Then we'll see what's up," I said calmly. So the police made everyone leave, and we talked about what was going on. My aunt was upset, so that pissed me off. "Tanny," I said, "let me take you home because I don't want you around this bullshit. I need to handle this."

"Stan, please don't do anything crazy. You're doing good now, and you don't need this. Cam isn't doing anything for himself at all." She was right, but in my mind this was my family. I took her to her car, and she said, "Please be careful."

I was going to call one of my little men, but I didn't think this would be anything big. I went back to my aunt's house and we got in my van to go find these boys. It was Montgomery County, so to me, this was some county bullshit. I thought my cousin was going to knock this nigga out and we'd leave. Needless to say, that wasn't the case. When we pulled up where they were, we saw the guy running to my van with a gun. He immediately started shooting. My reaction came so fast, I didn't even have time to think. Before I realized what was happening, I was shooting with bad intent. This bitch got scared and ran back to the car. They were pulling off as he dove in the back seat to keep from getting left. I was so mad that I took off behind them still shooting. I could see the holes in the car and the window was shot out. We went for miles, and then got to a big four-way intersection. They got stuck in traffic, so I got on the shoulder to ride up on them. They saw me and pulled out on the shoulder in front of me to keep me from riding up on their car. I knew they were scared because they then ran a light and were almost hit head on. The other cars locked brakes to keep from hitting them. I decided to go behind them through the light. Cars were blowing their horns and locking brakes. Now God saved them because just as I got up on the car, they lay in the seats and I pulled up to shoot. The gun jammed. I knew that this was a sign, so I pulled off, and then they ran the next light and fled.   They next day was Sunday, and I woke up thinking about what would happen if they went back to Cam's house. I went over to another spot and got my Tec-9. I was going to leave it with Cam so that if they returned he would be ready. As soon as I pulled up, a police car that had been sitting in the complex put the lights on me, and I knew it was on. My mind said to run, so at first I kept going. For some reason, I then decided to pull over. I had a Tec-9 and my Glock 9. The Tec was in a duffle bag in the rear of the van. The Glock was on my waist. The policeman walked up with his gun out. "How are you doing today, sir? I need you to turn the vehicle off now," he said calmly. Now this usually means that it's a problem. "I got a report about a van having a shoot-out yesterday, and this van fits the description. Do you know anything about that?"

"No, sir, I sure don't," I responded.

"Well let me get your driver's license and registration and sit tight for me." I knew he was going to call for backup. As soon as that thought left my mind, I heard the sirens. Police were everywhere; they knew what had happened and that I was involved. Now his ass came back to the car with a new attitude. "I need you to step out slow and walk to the rear of the vehicle," the officer said. I had taken my Glock and placed it in a tray under the passenger's seat. "If we don't find any weapons, you're free to go." They tore up my van and found the Glock. "Mr. long do you know anything about this gun?" he asked.

"No, sir."

"So could you tell us what's in the duffle bag and save me some trouble searching?"

"I don't know; it's not mine," I answered. Needless to say, they opened it and found a Tec-9 with extended 34 round clips in the bag.

I was on my way to jail now. "After being booked and processed, do you want to give a statement for me today?" the officer asked.

"Officer, I just want to call my lawyer. I don't give statements," I said.

"Okay, I wanted to give you a chance. You can take it now or do the time, its fine with me."

I never said another word until it was time for my phone call. Mr. Baritz was my lawyer. He was a Jew and he was a bad mothafucka. The problem was I had no bond. They said I was a threat to the community, so they didn't want to release me. I waited for a week, and they reduced my bond to $500,000, then to $250,000. I waited a total of two weeks, and the bond was $100,000. I then paid the $10,000 to get out on bond. The whole time I was thinking I should have listened to Tanny. I was going through all this shit for ten ounces of weed that I had nothing to do with. Then I found out Cam lied and really owed the mothafuckas the money. Now I was mad as hell. Everyone I knew was doing something illegal, and I wanted so badly just to live a regular life. The case got very costly because I had other gun charges. They thought I was gang related. Now I was about to lose all that I had hustled for in a blink of an eye. I was home on bond and facing at least ten years in prison. Life sure could take a turn for the worst pretty fast in DC. Trouble wasn't ever hard to find. People were disappointed in me because I was doing the right thing for once and let myself go backwards. I decided to stay to myself because I needed time to think.

At the time, I had an apartment in Virginia. It was a good place to get away. I found myself spending time there. My mother was so worried I was going to get in more trouble; she seemed to call me every five minutes. I understood why she was that way. My lifestyle had worried her to no end. Tanny tried to come back, but I didn't trust her anymore. I had spent lots of cash on my store already, and now I had to spend more on a lawyer that wasn't cheap. He wanted twenty thousand to start my shit. He said that because of my prior gun charges they wanted me in jail. I also did the shooting in a mostly rich, white area, and the judge took it personally. He said it was a reckless act that could have gotten people killed. In my heart, I realized he was right.

Meanwhile, I was trying to keep things together at the store. This was around the end of 1994. I had lost two of my best friends to this game, and now it seemed liked I was being pulled back in. I needed to make about fifty thousand really fast. The game was calling my name again. I called my connect and told him I needed to talk. I had a feeling that had never come over me before. I felt as though something was going wrong. I kept hearing my grandmother's words in my mind—"The Lord sees everything you do, Stan, even at night," she would say. The police were keeping an eye on me, and I knew it. I got rid of my cell phones and got new numbers. I kept a throwaway at all times.

I went to see my connect, and he threw me ten bricks to help me get back on my feet, but he told me that he felt like I should take it easy. "You're getting lots of attention, and it's not good, Stan. The streets are talking, and you're the conversation of the day. They know you paid cash for the store, and you still have a Benz 300 CE and a truck. You need to slow down so you won't make me hot," he said. He advised me to leave the shooting situation alone. He said it would only bring me more attention from the police. What he didn't realize was that the driver and a passenger were turning state on me. I wasn't having that because it meant jail time for me. They were the state's only witnesses, so I couldn't let them come to court. The driver was a white female that Cam knew, so I had him pay her a visit. The other witness was this fake-ass dude that was supposed to be Cam's boy. After a little persuasion, they both decided not to show up in court. Their DA was mad because they changed their testimony. He called me back down and said I was tampering with state witnesses, but he couldn't prove I had seen or talked to them, so he had no case.

The state still gave me two years probation because of my prior charges. They really wanted to lock me up, but God spared me once again. Around this time, I met a young lady named Rasheeda who was a road manager for Tanya Blount, a great singer who was about to sign with Bad Boy. I started traveling with them and having more fun. I promised myself that these ten bricks were my last run. I was tired of selling drugs. Rasheeda was not like other women I had dated. She didn't want me selling drugs and she spoke about positive things. She came to my store one day with Tanya and gave me a poster that Tanya had signed to me. She had a Bible in her hand and gave it to me. This was a first, but for some reason I felt that I needed it. She said, "Stan, you're a great guy, but the way you're living, you're going to hell or jail." She was crazy, but she meant well, so I didn't take it personally. We didn't date long, but we remained good friends.

My crew was glad to know that I had work again because they really needed me, but the whole thing just didn't feel the same as before. I knew my time was running out. I had been selling drugs for years and was considered a king pin. I knew I had to make good on my money if I wanted to get out soon. The store was doing better now, and I had hired a young lady to work for me. I sold the ten bricks and paid my lawyer off. Now I was focused on the store again. Some of my so-called friends seemed to be jealous of me. They didn't want me out of the game. They were stuck, and they seemed to want the same fate for me. They would always call to see when I was getting more bricks, but that was it for me. This one cat had been friends with Keedie, but I never did business with him. He started coming to my store asking for drugs. He wanted me to front him a half brick. Pee was his name, and I never trusted his ass, so I always blew him off. "Pee, I don't have no half brick, man. I'm out of the game now, so I don't know what to tell you," I said.

"Man, nigga, you can get me some work, man; I know you got connects," he said angrily. He was acting like the police had sent his ass. I started getting hang ups at my store every day. I felt like this shit wasn't right, but I wasn't hustling, so I paid it no mind.

Around this time, I met a young lady name Cookie. She was older but sexy. She had a little girl around two, but I really thought she was cool. We got along great because she was very funny. She also had a very sexy way about her. She was light brown with a slim build. I wanted to get to know her better, so we started spending time together. She had her own home and car. I was thinking about relocating, so I didn't want to get too close to anyone. I wanted a new start where no one knew my past. In Maryland, no matter what I did, I was known as a drug dealer. My past was always haunting me. She was just out of a marriage, so she wasn't trying to get serious either.

    This was close to my twenty-eighth birthday and life was getting more serious. I was making plans to go to Atlantic City for my birthday and have some fun. It was coming on a Friday. I wanted to stay the weekend. Friday came, and I wanted to be out early since it was my day. Anthony, my homeboy, had told me the day before that he wanted me to deliver some clippers to him before I left for Atlantic City. Some guy was standing in front of the bank right in front of my store. The bank wasn't open, so it struck my attention, but then I let it go. I told Tisa, the young lady working for me, to watch the store while I made some deliveries. I went over to Anthony's Barber Shop to sell a few pairs of clippers. After jokes and a few words, he gave me some green for my birthday and I was out. I went straight back to the store because I was trying to get to Atlantic City before there was a lot of traffic. When I arrived, I was feeling uneasy, but I didn't know why. Tisa said the phone had been ringing with hang-ups all morning, so I took off my coat and started talking to Tisa. As I looked up, a dude walked into the store quietly. "Can I help you, man?" I asked. He didn't say anything. Then he turned his back to me. I was about to ask again when he spun around and put a gun in my face.

    At first, I thought it was my man playing a joke, so I didn't move. "Come away from the fuckin counter!" he yelled out. I was frozen with disbelief. Then I quickly got angry. "Don't make me shoot your bitch ass," he said. Seconds later, three other men came in wearing masks. They snatched the phone cord and tied us up in the back. Now I was thinking, *who sent these dudes and why?*

    "I'm not going to repeat this shit, so tell me where the fucking money is," one of them said.

    "I don't have any money except in the register," I said.

"Don't make me kill your stupid ass." He then started to whip me with the gun.

One guy stooped down and whispered to me, "Stan, man, if you don't give us the money, I'm going to let them kill you!"

"I don't have any money," I kept saying. If they were going to kill me, they were going to still be broke. That was my thinking.

"Shoot his ass!" one of them yelled out loud. "Fuck him. He think we playin, so kill his ass."

This was getting bad, so I said, "I'll take you to some money if you let me up."

They tried to cut off my left pinky finger with a pair of wire cutters, but I pulled my hand back. After this, they let me up and said, "You're going with us." I had just said a prayer in my head right before that. God was with me the whole time. They drove my van to the back door and forced me into it. Now I knew if they took me, I was going to die. A voice in my head was telling me not to get into the van. As they put me in the van, the nigga tried to close the door with his gun hand. There were two guys outside, one in the driver's seat, and the one with the gun. As he tried to close the door, I kicked him in the chest and knocked him down. From the jerking, my hands had loosened the cords. I then ran to a grocery store up the street. "Stop before I shoot you in your head!" the driver said. There was no way I was going to stop. Tisa was still in the store, tied and face down. She was crying and shaking. I felt bad for her. They were going to shoot her first because they thought she was family. I grabbed the phone, called the police, and then ran back to the store to see about Tisa. When I arrived, the police were everywhere. They were searching my store for drugs, not for a crime of robbery. I threw all their asses out, and they refused to do a report. They said I wouldn't cooperate with them. I couldn't find Tisa, so I went next door to the barber school.

Everyone screamed when they saw me. I hadn't seen myself yet, so I looked in the mirror. I looked like a monster; my head was swollen and bleeding. I was so mad that I didn't feel any pain. Tisa was shaking and yelling. I then called a few of my homeboys to come down. I told them what had happened. They came down with guns out looking to get busy. This was a bad time for me. I never thought anyone would try me, because I was connected. I had been sleeping.

Now this shit definitely put a twist on things. Just as I thought I was clear of the bullshit, here I was again. I was really mad because for once I was trying to be out the game. I was even reading the Bible that Rasheeda had given me. It was starting to change my way of thinking. Why was this happening now of all times?

My homeboy Miles came down the next day to help me clean up the store. He wasn't one of my close dudes, but who the fuck do you trust now. I realized that someone I knew must have done it, but who could it be? It was time to lay low and find out who was involved. I didn't trust anyone after that day. Everyone was suspect in my mind. My so-called friends seemed happy because they were struggling with me not selling them drugs anymore. This made me think it had to be one of these them. I got closer to my homeboys that I knew were down and then quickly cut others off. I kept my eyes open. Miles was a cool dude and proved to be a friend. He told me a lot of valuable information. The streets were talking. Some of the suspects quickly surfaced. It's hard to look at someone who tried to have you killed and not blank out on them. That shit took strength I didn't know I had. I felt most fucked up about this because it all happened on my twenty-eighth birthday. God had spared my life once again, and I was thankful but also tired of all the bullshit.

Soon after that, my mother asked me if I cared whether I lived or died. My answer was no. I looked at life in a strange way. Most of my friends were already dead, so I felt like I had already cheated death. It was strange, but I never thought I would live to see thirty years old anyway. Most of my homeboys were dead or in jail by thirty. Mom cried when I responded to her question as a fool would. It tore her apart.

Two weeks went by, and I received a call from my man Poo. "Hey, man, I need to holla at you about something. The streets are talking, and you're the talk," he said.

"What are they saying, man? I got a lot on my plate, so I don't have time for no bullshit."   "You know Moe is dead, right?" he asked.

"No I didn't know that. How'd he die? What happened to the nigga?"

"That's what I need to talk to you about. We need to meet now," Poo said.

"Okay, meet me at Houston's because my ass is hungry and we can rap."

I met with Poo, and he began telling me how people said I sent some dudes to kill Lil Moe and shoot two other niggas. "They said they walked up on Moe and shot him in the forehead. Everyone thinks it was a hit from you," he explained.

"Man, I didn't even sit down about that shit yet because I was still putting this shit together. I can't lie to you—his ass had to go, but I didn't do it."

Moe's death made me really hot because everyone thought I killed him and his man Pete came to see me about it. He was nervous, so I knew his ass had something to do with it. Pete's father came in my store the next day to buy a can of hairspray, dressed in all black looking funny in the face but he was really coming to see who was in my store. I locked his ass in my store so he wouldn't be able to let anyone in. I had a buzzer put on my door after the robbery. When I let him out, he wasn't too comfortable. I told him I was going to kill every nigga involved. It was a dude at the corner phone booth with a black duffle bag on his shoulder. I knew this was an attempted hit, but I had two pistols on me, so I didn't give a fuck. His dad quickly gave a hand signal, and the dude started walking off slowly. I wanted to shoot his ass then, but everyone was outside in front of the barber school.

Next, I got a call from the detective about Moe. I called my lawyer, and we went down to talk. It turned out to be about Moe and another dude that I didn't even know. They also informed me that Pete's father was dead. I didn't know that until they told me. They had been watching my store since the robbery, so they thought I had something to do with everything. My prior gun charges didn't help my situation at all. My lawyer got me past this, but I knew it was time to leave. I had to shake this heat.

A few months later, I sold my store. I just wanted to be gone, so this was my chance. I left for Charlotte without many people knowing. I wanted to make a new start. I didn't even tell many women, so it was like I just vanished from the city. Things had started to change for me. I was growing up and now valued my life. I felt a sense of worth for the first time. My uncle, who had helped raise me, had gotten locked up for selling drugs and was doing ten years in prison. I always talked to him and tried to send him money. He was always in good spirits whenever he called. He was due home in 2002, so I often thought of him.

I went to Charlotte and finalized my papers to move in. Things were going okay, but Charlotte was very slow. I partied a lot to keep busy, but my mind was on Maryland. I had my barber's license, so I started to cut hair in a shop that a friend hooked me up with. Being in North Carolina gave me plenty of time to think. I thought about my life and why I was still alive. All of my friends were dead or doing life. Some had ten or fifteen years in prison. God had spared me for something, but I just didn't know what. I was starting to realize that I had a purpose. This girl Cookie that I had met was starting be on my mind. She was funny and didn't ask for much of anything. That was a change for me with women. I was starting to want to settle down and have a family. That was one of the things on my mind. I wanted a new life, but I didn't quite know which way to go. Finally, I decided to talk to God. I had never made that decision before. I knew God, but we hadn't talked in quite awhile.

    DC was full of murderers and thieves, so it was a place that had hardened my heart. I didn't realize this until I moved away. People were not as tough and hard in other places. In North Carolina, people would talk to you even if they didn't know you. This was strange to me, because in DC they would just look at you. DC is a very tough city, and showing love is unheard of. Saying what's up means you're weak or just visiting. DC is a place all of its own. Its home to go-go music and PCP. It's also the murder capital. The women are as live as you're going to get and very straight up. It's a real place with people who are going to keep it real. That part I really missed. DC has a very strong heartbeat, so to up and move away wasn't easy even in bad times. I was used to drama, but something told me I made the right choice. I started visiting the strip clubs because the girls in North Caroline were funny acting. If you're not in the clique they know of, then you get no play. This was some country shit to me, but hey what could I do. Tiny was still around, so she would come to visit from time to time. A few others would fly in to see me. That's what kept me grounded.

I started driving down to Atlanta because it seemed more my speed. The women in Atlanta were cool. It was slow, but not like North Carolina. I never got to like North Carolina because it was too far from what I knew. I was cutting hair, but there was no money to be made. I was starting to get tired of it fast, and I was getting reports from DC about the murders, and niggas were starting to talk. I was homesick. My man Boxcar was making money with dump trucks. He had been saying that I needed to get one. He showed me a check for $3,500 for one week. He then told me that his Uncle Shelton was a broker for the trucks. After six months in North Carolina, I was bored as shit. I knew something had to change quickly. I couldn't take the lifestyle any longer. I started going back and forth to DC again. My money was going down the drain because I didn't have much going at the time. I had to think of something.

I made a promise to God not to sell cocaine anymore, so now I had to settle for weed. Rhondell hooked me up with some New York dudes who wanted pounds. I was back in the streets again. The city was dry, so I was thinking about my promise, but I knew inside that it wasn't a smart move. I already had heat on me from before, so I stayed with the weed. I had a guy from who would buy twenty pounds a week, and Rhondell set me up with some guys that would get about thirty pounds. Since God and I had been talking, I felt more convicted every time I did something in the streets. I knew deep down inside I had to make a change, so I started an entertainment company called Short Stack Entertainment. This was in 1996. It was based in Charlotte. I started to promote parties, and so it went okay. The money was all right, but the people I met and the fun I had was the best. I was still home sick and thinking about how to get back to DC. The dump truck thing was heavy on my mind. I called my man John who had a truck to get more info. He told me to come home for a week and ride with him. I went home to Maryland and rode with him on his dump truck for a few days to see if I would like it. It seemed fun because a lot of my friends had bought tucks and they were all one big family. They rode and played on the CB's all day.

I still had an unanswered question: why when I was readying the Bible did God allow the robbery to happen to me? My cousin Pat was from the streets and had given her life to God, but even she couldn't say. During the times when I never thought of God, I didn't face these types of problems. I think Satan was mad at me for jumping the fence on him. He was mad because I was thinking of God now for the first time. I couldn't think of any other reason.

I had been in North Carolina for about eight or nine months and I hated it, so I packed up and moved back home to Maryland with my mom. She had mixed feelings about me moving back. It was sort of bittersweet. She was afraid that I would get in trouble with the streets again. I knew she only wanted the best for me, so I never said much back to her. Now the thing was I didn't have a job, so I needed someone to sign for my dump truck. I started talking to my mother about the business. She was all for it because this way she knew I wouldn't be selling drugs. I talked to other people who had trucks already. They told me to make sure I had work lined up before I bought a truck. They all agreed that you don't want your truck to sit because you won't make a dime. I was a risk taker, so it was just another chance at success for me.

I didn't tell many people that I was back because I was looking to have a new life. A place called Brandywine Trucks had a deal on a freight line dump truck. I went down to look at the truck and it looked like a good one. I knew absolutely nothing about dump trucks, but I knew I needed to win at something. John had gotten me a driver, so I was ready to get into it. I didn't even have a commercial driver's license at that time and had never driven a dump truck. John had the driver come pick my truck up for me since I couldn't drive it. He was a good dude, so he agreed to help me get my CDL. I didn't know at the time, but the driver turned out to be a crack head. John had set up a job with his broker, Mrs. Green, and my driver didn't show up for the job. Now here I was—the first job with no driver and no driver's license. I called John and said, "Man, this crack head motherfucker didn't even show up for the job. Now what am I supposed to do, because if I don't show, it's going to look fucked up for my truck in the future."

"Okay," he said, "I'm going to not go to work today and come help you on your truck. I'm going to ride, but I'm not driving—you are."

"Man, you know I don't have a CDL, so what are you saying?" I asked laughing.

"Man, fuck it, we're going to work that shit out. You'll be all right; just take your time and we'll listen to the CB for the DOT police. If they come on the job, then I'll drive, but—shit—you need to practice anyway, so I'll meet you at your truck at 6:00 a.m."

I had no choice if I wanted this to work, so I was nervous but game. I had been driving around at night on my truck to get practice, so I knew how to drive but had never picked up or dropped a load before. He met me at the truck, and we left for the job. I did everything right until it was time to get loaded. I had never backed up a damn truck under a loader before. The guy signaled for me to come back, so I did, but I was about a whole dump truck away from the loader operator. He just sat there and looked at me. Niggas were laughing, including my man John. They were on the CB talking shit, but I didn't even care. I just wanted to get it. Finally the operator rolled over with the bucket up in the air and just dumped the dirt any kind of way onto my truck. He was mad at me for not driving properly, so he rocked the trucked so bad, I thought we were going to flip. John jumped out and said, "Man, what the fuck did you do that for? Don't do that shit again. This truck is new, and so is the driver. He's just learning, so what the fuck are you mad for? It's your job to load the fuckin' trucks." The loader said he was sorry; he thought I was being an ass and didn't know I was a new driver. After that, the truck broke down on the job site. He had put too much dirt on, so when I went to dump, it broke the drive shaft. It wasn't looking too good for the first day. They had to sign me out early so I could get the truck fixed. Everything was crazy, but I kept my head up. It cost me about $400 to fix the truck. It was a very costly first day.

    It rained every day for about a week after that. This meant that my truck was now sitting. The little money that I had left was going fast. I had completely stopped hustling, so I was going broke. I hadn't been in that position since high school. I started hearing that voice saying, *Man, get your swag back. You need to call your connect and get back in the game.* It was starting to be a battle of the mind. I knew that wasn't what I wanted, but it wasn't looking too good for me.   The young lady Cookie had called me, and we started talking again. She was very supportive of me. She would bring me lunch and cook dinner for me. She didn't know much about my past, so she liked me for me. She even gave me money to help me with the truck. She was fresh out of a divorce, and I had a bad taste from my Cali girl, so we had lots to talk about. We started seeing more and more of each other and soon became close. She told me later that she heard rumors of me being a street dude but never held that against me. She started coming on the truck with me from time to time. I was a pro now at the driving thing, but I still had no CDL. I had been driving for about three months. Boxcar called me about his broker, but he said I needed to get my CDL before his broker would let me work for him. I started studying and was finally ready to take the test. I took it and passed. Now I was legit. The trucking business paid me $45 an hour, and it all seemed to be going back into the truck. Insurance was $500 a month. My note was about $600, and fuel was about $50 a day. This was a lot of overhead that I hadn't realized was part of the game. I started staying over at Cookie's more, so I parked my truck in her driveway. I was at a crossroad, and she really helped me get through it. We would just smoke weed and laugh all night long. Her daughter, Lauren, loved me, so it was all good. We were becoming slowly more than friends. For the first time, I was dealing with this one woman and not three or four. I must have been growing up, or I just couldn't afford them. Whatever it was, I was enjoying it for the first time. She was a real breath of fresh air. All the changes in my life made this an easy transition. The sex was crazy; I mean we had sparks flying off the bedpost. She showed me things that I hadn't experienced before. I would go over to her house, and it was as though we were out of town or on a vacation because we would drink Remy Martin and smoke weed and just have a great time. She was very fly and sophisticated. Cookie had class, so she taught me shit about music and art and those things. I felt that even though I didn't have money, I was finally alive.

    We started doing a lot more together, such as the time we got a suite at the Marriott in Baltimore. We had some drinks before we left and were freaking all the way down BW Parkway to the hotel. I can't say what we were doing, but trust me when I tell you it was freaky. As a matter of fact, this became the norm for us everywhere we went. She had a high sex drive, and so did I. Her mom would babysit so we could go out of town. One night she called and said she wanted to take me to a play the next day. The play was at some venue downtown in DC. Once again, we started playing in the truck I had bought, and before we knew it, we were in the parking garage at the play having crazy sex in the back of my jeep.

Chapter 6
The Transformation of a Gangster

Things were changing, including my friends, because I wasn't selling drugs anymore. I found myself starting to feel different too. God was talking to me, but I was afraid to listen. I never believed that God was for me because I didn't know anything about him. I thought that if you were a man doing the things I had done, then God couldn't possibly be for you. The church was making it seem as though I would be a hypocrite to come to God. Meanwhile, my life was really starting to take a turn for the worse, or so I thought. My money was going fast because I had a spending habit. I was used to buying whatever I wanted without thought. Now things were different because the drugs were out of my life. I made a promise to God that I would stop selling cocaine after he saved me from the attempted kidnapping. I knew who had saved me, because in DC you don't normally live to tell about being kidnapped or robbed.

Cookie was there for me, but it wasn't like me to ask for help. She was a single mom, so I felt I should be helping her. She took a new job at Bank of America downtown in DC, working for a top executive and making more money. We both were going through some changes, so we had a lot in common. She was off of a divorce and a single mom, while I had divorced the drug game and was going totally broke. My mother was a big help also. She let me stay with her for a while so I could get back on my feet. Bill collectors started calling me for the first time in my life. I didn't know how to handle it, so I would curse them out and hang up as though they were wrong. "Don't call my fuckin' house again. I'll pay you when I get the money," I would say. In the past, I had paid all of my bills as soon as they came in the mail. I didn't even look at due dates, so to not be able to pay at all was not the norm. I still had drug connects, but I was trying to keep my promise to God. For some reason, when your money goes low, you talk to God more than ever, or at least I did. Cookie and I decided to get an apartment together out in Crofton, Maryland. It was a very nice apartment, but there weren't many blacks, so we stood out like a sore thumb.

The truck situation was still up and down, so my money situation was just the same. I started looking for other options so I wouldn't have to depend on trucking. My weed connect was still good, but for me the game was over. I wanted to prove that I could make it without selling drugs. This would prove to be a tough road to take, and so it was. No more lavish trips, VIP parking, or ten-thousand-dollar rings. That wasn't what bothered me the most. I think my hang up was that I was looked at as regular and not as a big shot. My ego said I was losing, but for some reason I didn't give in to that. I'm a hustler by nature, so if it wasn't going to be drugs, then something to make money had to come up.

One day I was talking with one of my older homeboys who was selling clothes and handbags for a living. He was always fresh and always had money. He told me about the handbag game and how much he was making off the bags alone. I was impressed, so we went to New York the next weekend and got some handbags. I bought Gucci, Fendi, Louis Vuitton, Cartier, and more. I didn't know if it would work, but I was willing to try something new. I started getting calls all day once I hit a few shops with the bags. They would call for their customers as well as themselves. I would give discounts if someone referred me to others. Soon I was averaging $2,000 a week in bags. This wasn't what I was used to, but it was more than a job would pay. This was a good hustle, so I stepped up my game and added watches too. Now I was back to my old self and didn't have to sell drugs. I bought a truck and was on my way. Cookie was making money at her job, so things weren't so bad. The truck was not doing well at all, so I decided to sell it and get my money back. After a few months, I sold the truck and drove for the new owner who was another one of my homeboys. He gave me $15 an hour to drive, so it wasn't any money. I did that for about six months and then told him that I didn't want to do it anymore. I taught him how to drive so he didn't need a driver anymore.

    Now that I was going to New York more often, I started meeting people there who had wholesale plugs on the clothes. I started buying shoes, hats, and socks along with the watches and handbags. This was my new hustle. I was all over DC, Maryland, and Virginia. I did this from about late '97 until around '99. Around that time, Cookie started thinking of relocating to Charlotte because her boss was being transferred back to North Carolina. I wasn't sure about that because I had lived there already. Also, a young lady named Tanya had come into the picture. She was dark skinned with a beautiful face and smooth, pretty skin. Women were my weakness, and she made it hard for me. Cookie found out about me seeing Tanya and started to be in my business. She would play on Tanya's phone and also follow me to her house. That led to a break up for me and Tanya, but it also started Cookie cheating, or so I thought. I wasn't sure if I should leave. I had just bought a boxer dog named Hydro. He was like my son, so this also made me to think. I kept him at my mother's house, so I had to have a place that would take him if we moved. I named him Hydro because I used to smoke (hydroponic) weed, and on the way from picking him up, I was smoking in the car with my windows up and he almost died. This gave him the name Dro. Cookie said it would be best for both of us to just leave DC. I said that she should take the job and go there first, and I then would go there soon after.

    She decided to do so and found an apartment that took dogs. Because she was a bank employee, they gave her a big discount on the rent. Now that was cool because my dog was very close to me. I got him at six weeks old and trained him myself. He was like a person. This dog did everything but talk. He not only earned the name Hydro from weed, but also because he would piss every time he was going to be in trouble. If you cooked anything BBQ, he would go crazy and dig in the trash. I would tear his butt up for it, but he would do it anyway. He would piss as soon as I got home and called his name after going in the trash. He would also get mad and drag my clothes all over the house if I didn't do what he wanted when I left. He could tell the scent on my clothes and knew it was my stuff. He was the smartest dog I've ever seen in my life. One day we had a cookout at my mother's house and as soon as I put down my plate of BBQ, Dro ran up and tried to eat all of it. He even ate my Mac & Cheese. When the cookout was over, we bagged up the trash and later Dro got into the trash and ate some old potato salad. It made him so sick, he was stiff legged. This was one of many of his trips to the doctor. He was also the funniest dog in the world. He loved Lauren (Cookie's daughter) so much, he would growl if you fussed at her around him. He became a real part of the family.

So I went down to Charlotte to help Cookie get moved in and to look at the place where we would be living. Charlotte had stepped it up tremendously. It was so different that I didn't even recognize it. It was still slow, but not like in 1995–96 when I was there. Plus, having Cookie with me made it a lot easier. I moved her to Charlotte in November 1999, and I didn't move down until February 2000 after tying up my business in Maryland. Things were going fine except my money was gone and I only had a few thousand dollars to my name. I was smoking weed heavily to ease my mind. God was still speaking to me and was getting louder, or I was listening more; either way, it was getting to me. After a little partying and hanging out, I decided to settle in and find myself. I told Cookie I felt empty and needed to find myself. For some reason, every time I went to pick up the Bible, people would call or something would stop me. It felt like Satan was sending people to stop my new path. Meanwhile, Cookie and I were enjoying life even though I had no job. Actually, I had a job as a barber with my homeboy Corwin at his shop, but I was making nothing. It was very humbling, but for the first time, I was not on the edge. Some days I sat in the shop and made just $15 or $30 dollars. I was really only trying to meet new people.

    Charlotte dudes had already heard about DC guys, so they were kind of nervous about me at first. Rhondell helped me to get in with these guys, and I started meeting more people all the time. My cousin Amp was there, s o we started hanging out and it was all good. It felt good to have family around even though I hadn't been around him in years. He knew quite a lot of people, so he hooked me up. Now I was meeting people fast and I was becoming popular. Charlotte dudes were different from my homeboys because they were trying to have an identity. They mostly sweated New York guys and tried to be them. We never cared about another city; we only cared about what we wanted to do. DC guys have their own identity, and I seemed to gain respect by just being from there. My cousin had changed to a Charlotte guy, but I didn't care as long as he didn't try to change me. The same guys that my cousin was sweating actually started to sweat me. They knew I was not cut from the same cloth as my cousin, so his friends became my friends.

    About a year or so went by, and I wanted a house for my dog. We found a house that was rent-to-own and not far from the apartment. It was three bedrooms with two and a half bathrooms and was very nice. Things were starting to look up for us. Lauren didn't have to change schools, so it was all good. The house also had a fenced-in yard for Hydro. I found a new hustle selling barber supplies out of the truck. I still had connections from the barber supply store that I owned in Maryland. I would ride around and sell clippers or wait at the shop for a call and deliver them. This worked for a while, but North Carolina dudes were cheap and didn't want to spend any money, so eventually I stopped doing that. I decided to take a real estate class, since I had already started looking into property in Maryland and DC. I first had to pass the test, so I studied really hard but then failed by four points. I was determined to pass, so I kept on studying. People at the barbershop would hate on me and make negative comments about me and the real estate. They were haters in Charlotte for sure. I never had seen black people hate on each other like I saw in Charlotte. They hate on you as soon as you try to do something that they don't think is possible. Anyway, I was not going to quit until I had a license. Time went on, and I failed the test four more times. My mother said to me, "Stan, why don't you just get a regular job?" I told her that a regular job is for regular people. Even she never knew how determined I really was. Now the state board recognized that I already had sixty hours of class work from Maryland. All I needed was the six more hours of books, so I had no problem getting that part. It was the state board that was giving me all the trouble.

  Cookie helped me study at night, and I was determined to pass the next test. The state board said that they had to return my certificate and if I didn't pass this test, then I had to go back to school. I took the test again and passed. My birthday was the next day. It was time to celebrate because this was the start of a new beginning for me. Cookie was happy for me, and times were starting to be good. We had ups and downs, but we were hanging on. I had met a whole new set of people in real estate, and it was a welcomed change. I got involved right away with investment property. That was my main goal in real estate. Charlotte was on the rise, so there were plenty of opportunities for investing. I met a guy in class who told me about some builders who would do these types of deals. It would soon prove to be some valuable information. I started trying to find people with a good score who wanted to make money in real estate. It didn't take long for me to put a team together. I always had this passion for the real estate game, but now that I had been trained for it, I was ready. Every day, I would talk to people about real estate deals.

Soon I was ready for my first big deal. I met a builder who had connections in Charlotte but couldn't move his property. Dave was his name, and he was a complete redneck. The only thing we had in common was that we were two men who were trying to make some money in real estate. I knew right away that he wasn't going to invite me over for dinner, but that was fine as long as he could make me some money. He had four properties that he wanted to sell, but he was stuck. I told him I would take the property for what he owed the bank. He agreed and so now I had to find a buyer out of my team of investors. I had never done a deal in my life with houses, but I had learned how to negotiate. The street teaches you that skill almost immediately. So now it was time to put the plan into action. I called up my engineer friend who wanted to invest. I told him I would give him twenty thousand per house if he bought four houses. One house already had a tenant in the property with a positive cash flow. This sealed the deal, and so we made it happen. I walked away with about twenty-five thousand. This was fair, so we all won. Dave sold his houses, I made over five thousand per house, and my investor made eighty thousand. This was my first deal in the real estate game but definitely not the last. I started getting more clients and lenders and builders. This was starting to look great.

Cookie and I weren't getting along as well. We still had trust issues and other problems. My mother was still in Maryland, so we would talk from time to time. Most of my friends were all new. Cookie started doing things that I didn't approve of, but we were still together. I gave her money to get on her feet. After all, she had been down for me all the while. Now I still had these thoughts of reading the Bible and getting grounded, so finally I had some down time and started to do just that. I thought, *I've tried everything, now let me try God.* More than real estate or anything else, this would change me.

Once we had gotten settled into the new place, I started to fix it up. I went to a retail store to get a dresser to put in Lauren's room. Matthews, North Carolina, was a real redneck area for the most part. So when I to the retail store, I seemed to stand out and felt like all eyes were on me from the moment I walked in. I found a dresser that was perfect for Lauren's room, but it was too heavy of a box for me to pick up without help. I went to the old apartment to get this dude Greg to help me out. He came back to the store with me and we looked around a little and then went to the register. When it was my turn to get rung up, the lady asked me, "Sir, can I see some ID please?"

"Why do you need my ID if I'm paying with cash?" I asked.

"Well, sir, someone called up front and asked me to be sure to see your ID," she said. "I'm not showing you ID, so call your manager to the register," I said. Now I knew that I was in a redneck city because I felt like it was the 1920s. Coming from a 90 percent black city, this was all new to me. So anyway, the manager came out—and she was black, by the way. "How can I help you, sir?" she asked.

"Well I was trying to buy a dresser in cash, and the cashier wants to see my ID. Is this a store policy to ask for ID when cash is being paid?"

"Well, sir, if it's a large ticket, then yes," she stated.

"A large ticket shouldn't matter if it's cash because what would you match my ID up with?" I asked. "Plus this is a dresser for $275, so what's large about this ticket? I really need you to tell me."

"Sir, I'm going to go ahead and have her ring you up anyway this time," she said with an attitude.

"No that's not what we're going to do," I said. "You're trying to tell me that this is a store policy, and I know this is just racial profiling, so since you could not rectify this as a manger, I will have to sue your store. I don't want the item, so just tell me your name and the cashier's name and I'm going to take it from here."

"Sure," she said, and she gave me her name and the name of the cashier.

I immediately called my lawyer in Maryland to talk about the case and he said I had one, so I contacted lawyers in North Carolina. I couldn't find anyone there who would take my case, so I decided to take matters into my own hands. I sat down and wrote to the corporate head quarters. I made it a certified letter. They responded immediately and tried to offer me a $250 gift certificate. This was some shit, especially for someone who never even shopped at the store. I told them that if they didn't get it right, I would no longer talk to them, but my lawyer would take over. They said they would refer my case to the claims division for better results. Long story short, I settled out of court for $10,000. This was much needed, so I was on my way. Now I realized that Charlotte was a place that looked at black people like they were all slow or second-class. Even the blacks looked at themselves as though they were still slaves. I didn't understand how this could be, but I knew for a fact that I wasn't having that. They quickly saw that all blacks don't just talk loud and say nothing.

Cookie and I had been talking about a magazine for a while, so now was the time since I had some change to work on it. We went right to work on setting up the magazine. We named it *Fetish* magazine. This name came about because I was known for my foot and hand fetish, so we decided to incorporate this into the magazine and talk about everything from fashion fetishes to car fetishes. The timing was perfect, and we immediately got great feedback from the public. Cookie found a printing company, and then we got a photographer and some models. I was in charge of the girls. Cookie quickly took over everything, even the girls. I got a seamstress, and we went to several stores and started to bargain with them. In exchange for promotion space, they allowed us to use their clothes as well as the storefront for the photo shoots. Everything was going very smoothly. We knew a guy who owned an art gallery, so we decided to put the promo party together using his gallery. We put a fashion show together to show off the clothes and hired a DJ. Now the buzz for the magazine became great. We got on the radio along with comedian Tommy Davis. Things were starting to look up for *Fetish* magazine.

We had one situation that put a damper on things for a moment. We called up Tuff Rider for Eva to give us an interview and she declined, but never mind that, her ass stole the name Fetish for her clothing line after we sent a copy of the magazine to her. That's how she got the name Fetish. We didn't have it copyrighted, so there wasn't much we could do. Anyway, the promo was finally finished, so now we were ready for the magazine promo party. We had free beer and wine and a VIP section. Everyone showed up, and the party was very diverse. Now Cookie had started feeling herself so she didn't give me much credit at all; in fact, my name was mentioned only one time in the book, for being in charge of the girls. I saw another side of her that didn't sit well with me. She started having an attitude with the girls and the seamstress. This left a bad taste in my mouth, so I decided to withdraw from the magazine. The party went well, but I didn't want to invest another dollar in that type of situation. We probably could have been very successful, but I saw that it was getting to her head, and we hadn't made a dime. I decided to just focus on real estate.

I came home to the new place and decided to sit down with my Bible and give God a try. I never thought that just reading a book could change a person's life, but I realized that this wasn't just any book. It seemed to bring me to a light; one that I didn't even know existed. I didn't know where to start, so I began with Genesis. I had started reading in Maryland, but after the robbery, everything seemed to have left. I always knew of God, but I never really knew God for myself. Now that I was in this new city and this new home, I felt that it was time. The words just seemed to jump off the page as I read them. I became engrossed in the Bible, and a light came to me as though I had been living in the dark all of my life. Actually, I had been. It's like I could hear God talking to me as I read the Bible. The people in the Bible seemed familiar to me for some strange reason. I wasn't very far before a man named Enoch came to my spirit. I was intrigued by him because as I read about the line of Adam, he was the only man who didn't die in the whole blood line, at least at that time. God was speaking louder to me than ever before.   Enoch made me have to stop and go to my computer to pull up his name. I found a *Book of Enoch* that was even more enlightening. As a matter of fact, it was so good that I rushed to Kinkos and made it a book after printing off 108 chapters. I read the whole book in only two days. After reading this book, I had no doubt that God is real. So I stood up after two straight days of reading and confessed to God that I knew he was real. There was definitely no turning back at this point. My eyes were open, and I loved what I was seeing. Maybe Mom had been right all along. Maybe God had been trying to get my attention and I just wouldn't listen. But how could God want to use me after all the drugs I had sold and everything else I was involved in before now? When I began to read more, I found that these were the men that God chose to use throughout the Bible. The church had this thing all wrong. It wasn't that you get right and then come to church, you come to church in order to get right. Anyway, I had a newfound relationship with God, but I wasn't perfect by far. My life was starting to take a turn for the better.

One day as I was driving with Cookie to go to Sam's Club, something spoke to my spirit and said, *turn right*. It turned out to be a new subdivision with houses that were just sitting. I could tell that the builder was in trouble, so this was my chance to make some money. I went into the model and talked with the onsite agent about the property. I was pretending to be a buyer and she showed me the property. As I was leaving, the Lord said to tell her the truth. Now this was starting to feel strange, but I was cool with it. I turned as my hand was on the door and said to the agent that I was really an investor and was interested in buying the properties, but I needed to speak with the builder. She quickly got him on the phone, and we set up a meeting for that Monday. I knew he was desperate because he was ready to do it on Sunday. I said Monday would be better. This was all new for me because normally I would have agreed to Sunday. God was starting to really change my heart. I was even more easygoing now. Monday came and we sat down to talk. I told him that I specialized in builder closeouts, which meant I would bring in investors to buy his properties if he would agree to a wholesale price. He quickly told me he was trying to close on the three houses standing and then he would allow the same on the other seven lots in the subdivision. We crunched the numbers and came to an agreement.

    I had other deals working in other subdivisions as well. I was still a rookie in real estate, but I was coming on fast. I had five deals on the table and now a new builder. I knew this was God. I was starting to see him working in my life. One of the deals was closing, and Cookie was getting one of the houses for herself. We agreed that we needed to go our separate ways, but we remained friends. It was God that told me to make that right. It was all clear now that he had been with me the whole time, good or bad. I closed my deals and made about $60,000. Life was great, and real estate was paying off. Now, instead of me buying the ranch, I decided to buy a home in the new Beckwith subdivision. It was about 3,000 square feet and had granite counters and marble fireplaces. It was a beautiful home. This was one of the three models. I got my investors together, and we made it happen. The builder gave me an excellent deal. I was really starting to make money with little to no effort at all. I had quickly built a reputation for being a closer. Some investors would not finish their deals, so builders were referring them to me. Money was coming really fast and I was living well. Things were good until one day I came home and my dog was having a seizure on the floor and couldn't respond. Hydro was like my son, so I rushed him to the animal hospital and they ran tests. I got a call around 1:00 a.m. from them saying I should come right away. He wasn't doing well and there was nothing they could do. It brought me to tears to see him just laying there hopeless. I told the vet to put him to sleep. That was the hardest decision I had ever made in my life. I sat in my truck and cried like a baby. Life seemed to leave my body for a time, and nothing really mattered. Even though I was making money again, life for a time just wasn't the same. I decided to move into my new home after having it freshly painted and landscaped. I always thought about the boxer dog named Hydro.

    Thanksgiving was coming up, and Cookie decided to ride with me down to my Aunt Lou's house in Virginia for the holiday. We had been rebuilding my grandmother's home because my mother felt that it was important, and so did I. My grandmother's home was near Aunt Lou's house, and we all had pretty much been raised there. Just to be driving to that home brought back many memories. Cookie and I discussed those memories on the way from Charlotte during the two-hour drive. She seemed to be intrigued by the way so many people could grow up in a house so small. One thing I remembered was that no matter how many of us were in that house, it was always filled with love. Don't get me wrong, there was plenty of drama to go around, but it all would end in love. Like any family, we had our bad times and some were much worse than others. Life was very simple in those days because no one really had much. Going to town was one of the exciting things we did, and that only happened on a Saturday. We would pile into grandma's Ford LTD and head to Danville. That was considered town even though there was only a K-Mart and small stores there. It didn't even have a mall, but we never missed any of that. Like they say, you can't miss what you never had. I often thought of my grandmother, so much so that I named my real estate firm after her. It was called G. Medley Realty. That stood for Georgiana Medley. It was all I could do at the time to make her name live on. She deserved it after all she did for my family. Grandma was the glue that kept all of us together.

    I rambled on and on to Cookie about my fond memories of my grandmother as we finally approached the house. "Man, so we finally made it and just look how good the house looks," she said.

"Yeah it does look good for being so old. They seem to have done a great job from looking at the outside," I said. So we pulled in the driveway and sat there for a few minutes. I just felt strange being back there, and all the memories from that small green house seemed to come alive. I could still remember the hog pen in back of the house and having to take the slop bucket down to the trough to feed the pigs. These memories were suddenly playing in my mind as we got out of the car. We walked up the gravel driveway to an open carport, which was the original from back in the day. The memories of us wrestling in the yard and playing tag team as though we were Rick Flair or Ricky Steamboat or Rusty Rhodes played in my head. I remembered jumping off the side of the porch on my cousin Jr. and hurting him, not realizing that what I had seen on TV wasn't real and was done by stunt men. We did them on each other for real. That was one way we created our fun. As I stood at the carport, I looked down the back of the house near the smokehouse where the meats would get cured and thought about the basketball goal made of milk crates with a wooden backboard nailed to a tree. The court was dirt that came from wearing away the original grass.

Next door was Brandon Chapel Church that we all grew up in and the graveyard that my grandmother and all of my family were buried in. The road, which had been forever a dirt road, was now freshly paved. The air was as fresh as ever and there was a sense of calmness. We decided to go inside for a look at the house to see how they had done. Entering the three-bedroom ranch with a basement, I noticed that the kitchen had been totally redone. All the appliances were new and modern. It was a far cry from what I could remember. I longed to smell those homemade biscuits and rice pudding my grandma used to make. They would put Popeye's out of business. We peeped into the small living room area that none of us could ever go into, and it was pretty much the same. The house had a strange feel that Cookie may not have noticed, but I certainly did. It felt like the walls were talking and I was trying to understand what they were saying. We ventured down the hallway that had fresh paint. To my right was a newly tiled bathroom that resembled nothing I could remember. The first thing that came to my mind was this red hot-water bottle that used to hang in the bathroom from time to time. Now that I was older, I realized that it really was a douche bag used for cleaning a female during her menstrual cycle. Sometimes Grandma used it to give out a beating or two. Every room seemed to tell a story.

To my left was the first bedroom, which was the one I slept in along with whoever else was there at the time. It looked the same. The first thing I thought of was going to bed and passing up dinner so that I wouldn't get a beating. Grandma would come in the room after cleaning up the kitchen and watching wrestling and tear my ass up. The next room was right next door and everyone stayed there also. I remembered my cousin Sheila sleeping in this room, and one day I walked in on her ass naked and was totally shocked. She didn't even seem fazed by it. "Boy, close that door and get out," was all she said. Finally the last room, which was in the center of the narrow hall at the end, was my grandmother's room. This room was full of memories of her. She would sit up in the bed and read the Bible every day of the week. Although her education was not much, she knew enough to read the word. Sometimes she would call me in to read something that she didn't understand. Other times, it was only to rub Ben gay on her aching legs. She was a very good woman with a strong will. All these things came to mind while walking through the house. I relayed these thoughts to Cookie as we walked along. "Let's go down in the basement and see how it looks. I wonder if they did anything down there," I suggested.

So we went downstairs and saw that it had changed a little, but not much. A room had been closed off that at one time was open. As soon as I got down there, I remembered when my two cousins and I got into a fight over air being let out of my new bike tires. They jumped me and pushed my face to the heater and my skin melted on one side as it stuck to the wooden heater. We all ended up getting the ass whipping of our lives.

My uncle Ice was on the run from the police, so he used to stay down there too. He would go out gambling and come home with thousands wrapped up in rubber bands. In that house, there was never a dull moment. Cookie sat and listened to my stories for a while, and then we headed back upstairs. She had a camera and was taking pictures the whole time. On the way up the steps, we decided we should go over to visit my grandmother's gravesite.

We said good-bye to the house, took the last picture of the kitchen, and were about to head out the door. *All of a sudden, black birds filled the ground as though they had just dropped from the sky. There were so many birds that we couldn't even see the grass.* I had never seen so many birds in my entire life. They seemed to be tied together because everything they did, they did in unison. "Cookie, do you see all these birds outside?" I asked as we looked through the screen door. She stood as if she was frozen, and so did I. In fact, she never even answered me. "Take a picture of them because it's amazing! Cookie, take the camera out and get a picture before they leave!" I yelled. It was as though she was in some kind of trance.

"Stan, I'm afraid to go outside on the porch because I can hardly move my legs," she said. I felt the same way, like something had my feet stuck to the floor the moment the birds landed on the ground. Finally after about three minutes, which seemed like forever, we tried to push open the screen door to go onto the porch for a better look. The birds rose up and then went back to the ground as though they were on a string. They made a loud roar that sounded like a quiet thunder. That frightened us even more. For some reason, those birds had a presence that you could feel inside. Cookie got the camera finally and snapped the picture. The birds immediately flew into the trees surrounding the graveyard. This was the strangest thing I had ever witnessed in my life. There were so many birds that the trees all turned black. As we walked toward the graveyard, the birds flew into the air, and then what happened next was totally mind-boggling. They started to do tricks that only trained birds should be able to do. I can't even describe it on paper because it looked like someone or something was commanding these birds. As we got closer to the graveyard, they seemed to fly away. We quickly noticed a huge tree that had the appearance of a giant man in the middle of the graveyard. We realized that all of the black birds were at the base of that tree piled up on top of each other. Now we knew that something strange and very, very different was going on with these birds. We slowly walked into the graveyard and visited the grave of my grandmother. We took pictures and stayed about thirty minutes. The birds remained at the tree the entire time we were there. As soon as we left, the birds all flew into the air in front of us, and then they all flew out of sight together.

  Cookie and I stood speechless for a while. When we got back into the car to leave, we noticed two iron black birds on the front of my grandmother's house, on the side of the front door, that resembled the ones we had just seen. I didn't know what to say, so we just drove off in silence. Finally, Cookie said, "What the hell just happened back there?"

"Cookie, for real, I can't tell you the answer to that, but whatever it was, it wasn't something normal. I have never in my life seen anything close to that. It didn't even seem real," I said.

"I know, that's what I mean. It seemed like a dream or something. That many birds and then they seemed to follow us and then wait on us."

"That's the same feeling I got. It was hundreds of birds all seemingly tied together. We got to get to Aunt Lou's house so we can tell them about what just happened. They're not going to believe this," I said. Cookie still seemed to be shaken by what had occurred. She had this blank look on her face the whole time I was talking.

We arrived at Aunt Lou's house and couldn't wait to tell them what had just happened. "Man, y'all are not going to believe what just happened to us at Grandma's house." Everyone was gathered around, so we told them from the beginning what had happened, and before I could finish the story, my uncle interrupted me and asked me if they were black birds. When I said yes, he looked at his girlfriend and told us that this was the same thing that had happened the day of my grandmother's funeral. He said that black birds came from nowhere and filled the trees during the funeral. My mouth dropped open because now it seemed to be getting even stranger. He said that they stayed until the funeral was over and then flew away.

I told them that we had taken pictures of the birds and we wanted to go home and get the pictures developed. We left the next day and went to get them developed at Eckerd's Drugs. We were so excited that we waited in the parking lot for the film to be developed. After one hour had passed, we went in and the pictures were finally ready. I paid for the pictures and then stood at the counter looking through all the pictures of the house until finally I came to the one of the birds. I stood as still as though I was dead when I saw what was in the picture. To my amazement, there was not even one bird in the picture. I couldn't talk, so Cookie got nervous and asked what was wrong. I could do nothing but hand the picture to her. She looked at the picture and saw nothing but dirt and grass and tree limb shadows. We both just stood there as though we were frozen. Not one black bird to be found. This was a moment that was just breathtaking, to say the least. I thought I had something to show everyone to prove that I wasn't going crazy, but now Cookie would be my only proof. We didn't know what to make it, so we went back to the car and sat down and just kept on looking at the picture searching for a clue as to what could have happened. The strangest thing of all was that when she first took the picture, something came to my mind that nothing would show up. I quickly dismissed the thought because that didn't make any sense at all.

    At that time in my life, I was searching for God and trying not to go left. This had become a battle for me. I had been reading on a regular basis, and so I had started acquiring many books about God. I decided to go home and try to find out just what birds meant. For some reason, I picked a book called *The Secret Teachings of Jesus*. The book explained that birds were a symbol for the spirit. That made sense to me. The part I couldn't figure out was if it was Grandma's spirit or the spirit of the Most High or both. What I did know is that you can't see spirit. It wasn't for everyone to see at that time, but for me, and Cookie was there only to be a witness to what had occurred. I was thankful that she was there because if it had just been me, then I may have believed that I was going crazy. I called Cookie to tell her what birds stood for and she understood right away. It was a sign that God was showing himself to me. The memory of that day has stayed with me ever since. I never really discussed it much, but it had everything to do with me wanting to write a book.

    I met up with Rhondell's uncle one day for lunch, and he said that a rich client from Brooklyn wanted to do some business in Charlotte, but he didn't have time to show him around. Now Al was rich himself, but he didn't think that I knew that. I guess that's why he didn't have time to deal with Mr. Land. He said he had never met the man, but he was a friend of his best friend in Brooklyn. I was very excited to meet with him because this was an opportunity for me to make some big deals. Al told me that this guy was older and very conservative but not to be fooled by that. He said that I should show him any house he liked because he definitely had the money. Finally I met Mr. Lane, and strangely his name was Joseph Land. If you read the Bible, you would know why this was strange. Joseph in the Bible had plenty of land. He was an older man, about seventy-two years old, and had a very distinctive look about him. Mr. Lane and I hit it off right away, and he quickly became like a mentor. Nevertheless, he was very picky and hard to please, so we would look at house after house after house. He was wearing me down somewhat, but I hung in with him. Finally Mr. Lane started asking about some investment deals, which was right up my alley because although I had my real estate license, I didn't show many regular properties. Investment deals had become my specialty. I showed him some of my deals and sure enough he wanted in. Mr. Lane actually started to put up money for some big deals that I had already worked on prior to meeting him. Charlotte had plenty of millionaires, so I had already begun to dream of very big possibilities before even meeting Mr. Lane. Now he began to help my dreams along.

    I learned a lot from him, and later as we spent more time, he became more of a father figure than an investor. He taught me a lot about money and how it works for you instead of you working for your money. This was a new idea for me because I had only a hustler's mind prior to meeting him. I learned quickly that how a man thinks has everything to do with what he does and who he becomes. Mr. Lane was a man who always thought big. So we did some deals, and Cookie, being a loan officer, made a lot of the deals happen. I was starting to live large, and one day while riding along, I saw this nice Mercedes sitting at a dealership. It had been placed up front so that you could see it from the main street. I decided to treat myself to a new car for all my so-called hard work. I thought, *you own your own firm and it's doing well.* I went in to talk to someone about the car and said to myself, *if they give me a good number on this car, then I'm driving it away today.* I always loved cars, especially Coupes. So I went in, and they made me an offer that I couldn't refuse, so you know what I did. Yep, I bought the Benz. Now I was already driving a Lexus and it was nice, but the Coupe was calling me and so I decided to answer.

    Mr. Lane started spending more time in New York because his regular job was as an engineer, and he had to work a lot. I was looking for a space to open an office for my firm because I felt it was time to expand. Now with a new Benz comes a whole new set of women, and as we all know, one of my weak points is women. I started meeting women left and right. It was kind of like the old days when I was selling drugs, except they were more quality women. After all, I was older now, so my taste in women was changing. I found a great location for the firm and rented the space. Everything was going great for me. I really wanted to find a woman so I could settle down and have a child and get married, but I was really enjoying this single lifestyle of not having to check in. Mr. Lane hadn't seen my office yet or my new car, so I wanted him to come down and be surprised.

My accountant, Mr. Free, was also a great friend who I had a lot of respect for. He became a big part of my business as well. He actually rented a space in my office for his tax business. He also worked for a company that had lots of used computers, so he hooked me up with some for my office. I had five office spaces, a reception area, and a supply room. I felt that God was doing big things in my life, so I was very thankful. The market in Charlotte was doing great and things were busy picking up. Mr. Lane finally came down to visit me, and now was my chance to tell him the good news about the office and the new car. Mom was also happy for me and helped me with a lot of things. She gave time up to help me pick out office furniture, and she gave plenty of advice about what to do as usual. Finally, I told Mr. Lane about my office, and he was proud. Then we met for lunch and I pulled up in my new Mercedes Benz. It wasn't quite what I expected when he saw the car. "Why did you go out and buy a new car now?" he asked.

"Well I thought it would be good for business and also because I've been working hard," I said. He was not only disappointed, but he was mad at me. I saw it all over his face. "That wasn't smart of you to do that, Stan. A car is a liability not an asset, assets are things that gain value in time; liabilities take away money in time. I thought you knew the difference by now," he said. "Well I didn't buy it new and I thought it wouldn't hurt for people to see a little success," I explained.

"You were doing just fine with your Lexus, so what made you think you needed a new car? Investors want to see how you handle your money so that they know how you'll invest theirs. This wasn't a smart investment because you lose money pulling away. Do you know that I drive an '89 4Runner that was paid for years ago? I have a $300,000 cashier's check in my pocket now. I'm going to buy a Hummer, but that's after years of investing, and

I'm seventy-plus years old now. I'm well established so I can pay cash for the truck. I thought you were smarter than what you just showed me."

I felt like I was about ten years old. At first I thought he just hated on me, but then why the hell would a rich man hate on a poor man. I respected him a lot, so I just listened and didn't say anything. Not a single word. I didn't know what to think, but one thing was for sure—I wasn't hungry anymore. I didn't realize it at that moment, but this was the beginning of the end of our relationship with business. Needless to say, Mr. Lane seemed really disappointed with my decision, but at the end of the day, I am a man and life must go on. I learned a valuable lesson, but the car wasn't going back. We didn't talk as much after that because I knew I wasn't going to put up with too much of that talk as though he was talking to a child. I gave him his respect, but I felt as though I had been disrespected. It's not what you say, but how you say it that matters. In my mind, he could have put it to me better than the way he did. So I moved on and found some people who were interested in working for my firm. I was getting back into the swing of things.

One morning, I was driving and received a call from the State Board in Raleigh, some redneck talking about how he needed to talk to me as soon as possible. *Oh shit, what have I done* is what quickly came to mind. When he called, I felt like he was the damn police the way he addressed me. So we arranged a day and time to meet. I told him to meet me at my new office on Independence Boulevard. As I arrived, this fucker was posted up waiting for me. I knew that this wasn't going to be a good day for me. "Mr. Long, good to see you," he said as I approached. "We need to talk about some of your real estate deals if you don't mind."

"Sure, let's step in my office and talk. What exactly do you need to talk to me about?" I said. So we sat in my office, and he pulled out a folder and started asking me about some deals I did with a company called Craft Homes when I first got started in real estate.

"So who is George Gordon and what do you know about him, because Craft is under investigation and your name is on some of the HUD statements as the broker." *Oh shit*, I thought as he talked. "We see that you have received some large commissions, and we consider this mortgage fraud. Are you willing to talk to me or do you want to give me your license for being unethical?"

"First of all, I'm not going to answer anything about anyone except Stan Long. If you want to know about someone else, you should go talk to them directly. I don't even know what this is about," I said with my attitude.

"Well basically we know that you're giving back money to buyers and you've also been receiving large payouts in commission. This is unethical, so if you can't talk about anyone, then I'm here to get your real estate license." He slid a paper to me and asked me to sign it.

I read the paper and realized he wasn't playing. "I'm not signing anything without talking to my lawyer first. As a matter of fact, I'm going to ask you to leave my office now," I said. "Well, Mr. Long, you've made your choice, so I'll give you some time to think and I'll be back in touch. You do know that I could easily have turned you over to the Feds, don't you?" he said as he took back his paper.

At that point, the street came out of me and I said, "Do whatever you have to do, but telling is not my thing." He got up red as a beet and tried to shake my hand as he walked out. Now you know damn well that wasn't happening after that news I just got from his racist ass. Others people had done this forever, but now that I was doing it, I got a visit. Charlotte was that type of city, so it didn't really surprise me. He said that he was giving me sixty days to tie up my business and then I needed to mail in my license. Now truthfully, I wanted to knock his ass out, but it wasn't going to help the situation. I wasn't going to give up that easily.

I quickly went home to call a real estate attorney. I set up a meeting and explained my case. I knew I didn't have a leg to stand on because I wasn't supposed to have a license anyway because of my record in Maryland and DC. If I went to a hearing, this was going to probably come up. In Charlotte, you don't need a license to own a firm, just to run one. After my lawyer explained that, she advised me to switch the broker-in-charge to someone I could trust. Also I had to change the name. It went from Long Real Estate Investments to G. Medley Realty. I've always been a fighter, so it was time to fight. I knew I could still do investment deals anyway. This one day changed my whole life as far as real estate. Now I had to change the whole game.

Chapter 7
Going to Atlanta and Meeting Peaches

A young lady who had agreed to work for me said she would become the broker in charge of the firm, but she had many requests. Basically she realized that my hands were tied, so she took full advantage. It would later prove to be a big mistake. One day while I wasn't at the office, Mr. Lane called and started talking to the young lady, Selma. She decided to tell him everything. I didn't find out for a while because he never let on that he knew about my situation.

During this time, I took a trip to Atlanta to see Joel Osteen and get away. I also had a longtime female friend named Teka who lived in Atlanta. She had always been down for me no matter what. Teka would always invite me to stay at her home whenever I visited, so this time I took her up on the offer.

I called her and said, "What's good, Teka, are you busy this weekend? Because if not I need a getaway and was thinking I would come stay at your place."

"Sure, Stan, you know you're always welcome. I'm not doing anything this weekend, so come down and we can catch up on old times," she said.

Now Teka and I were always great friends, but I have to admit we had messed around back in the day. We knew a lot of the same people, but for whatever reasons, I really trusted her. I finally arrived in Atlanta, and Teka came to meet me. She had a fly car and was living well.

"What's up, babe? Good to see you again," I said while giving her a hug.

"Good to see you too and you're looking real fly as usual," she said smiling.

We got to Teka's house, and it was a nice one, to say the least. I got settled and we talked about old times.

"Remember the time them dudes robbed you for forty thousand and you came to my house with a machine gun and blood all over you? I felt so bad for you, and you were mad as shit. I never seen you so mad before in all my life," Teka said.

"I know, and you were right there to hold me down and that's what I always loved about you. I knew if I couldn't trust anyone, I could trust you," I said with a grin.

We talked the whole night until we both fell asleep. Teka and I hung out the whole weekend, so I missed seeing Joel Osteen. I had a great time talking with her, and she gave me that much-needed break from reality. Teka had this way about her that always kept me in good spirits. I never knew why we didn't become a couple, but the friendship was great. I decided to take a trip to Lenox mall on my way out from Atlanta. This trip to Atlanta would prove to be a life-changing one. I met a young lady at Lenox Mall as I was leaving Neiman Marcus. Her name was Peaches. She was driving a BMW, and I pulled her over in the parking lot. We talked and seemed to hit it off. I started going to Atlanta often after that.

My mind completely left the business, and the business started going downhill. Selma was starting to take over as though it was her business. This young lady Peaches wasn't the norm for me, but there was something about her that drew me to her. Mr. Lane and Selma were busy plotting to steal my firm behind my back. I had asked him for financial backing because now I couldn't get money as I had before. All the time, he knew all about what was going on. Now the relationship grew quickly between Peaches and me. I quickly fell for this young lady, and I just couldn't figure out why. We had fun during the first few months of the relationship, but so does everyone in the beginning. They say you never really know someone for years and years. I usually do the six-week test. If they stay the same for six weeks, then that's how they are. This didn't work because we dated long distance the whole time. It's easy to be on good behavior for a short period of time. For some reason, I ignored all of the signs that told me to run. I think I was in a place where I wanted to settle down and have a child. Peaches had her own home, a nice car, and no children at all. She wasn't the party type, so that was also a plus. Everything seemed to be going fine at the time. We ate out a lot, which was fun for a while, but it got old after a few months. I waited to see if she would cook, but she never even offered. That wasn't a good sign. We ate out for breakfast, lunch, and dinner and I noticed that I was always picking up the bill. That was another flag that I totally ignored. We started to get into little riffs quite often. It was always some petty shit.

    About four months went by and—*bang*, Peaches was pregnant. I was happy because I wanted the baby, but she seemed sad even though we had planned for it. I started seeing things in her, but she was now pregnant and really starting to trip on me. For some reason, she would try to hide me when her family came from Florida to Atlanta to visit. I had never been treated that way, so I questioned it right away. This only led to more fussing and big blow-ups. I thought this was very strange because she always showed love but wouldn't allow me to see or meet her family. Finally, I met her snobby-ass sister. I knew she was fake the moment she spoke to me. This was the beginning of some really rough times for me. This relationship would prove to be a nightmare from hell. I didn't know it at the time, but Peaches' family had been controlling her ever since childhood. They treated her like she was fifteen years old. That was why she kept me away from them until she was pregnant. I used to press her to tell her parents about the baby, but she refused until she was four months pregnant. That was so they wouldn't try to make her get rid of the child through an abortion. She knew I wouldn't go for that anyway, so it became an instant battle between her crazy-ass family and me. They felt I wasn't good enough for their daughter.

In the meantime, I got a letter from Mr. Lane concerning my firm saying he would give me fifty thousand if Selma could have the last word over me, and he also wanted 51 percent of *my* company. I was having hard times, but not that hard. This time I lost my cool when we talked, and I used language that wasn't respectful. "Mr. Lane, I received your letter or offer and basically this is a bunch of bullshit. You think I'm going to give you full control over my firm for $50,000? Why the hell would anyone give more than 49 percent of the company? I'm not as slow as you may think. I don't know what the fuck Selma has told you, but her ass is fired and you don't ever need to call me again." He tried to interrupt, but I didn't want to hear any of that shit. "This is shit a stranger would do, not a so-called friend. Maybe I've made some mistakes, but you're not going to take my company or take advantage of me being down. You've never even seen this woman and you're making a deal against me with her. You think I'm that damn dumb to just give away everything I worked for because of my license? I'm smarter than you and Selma give me credit for, so keep your fuckin' money." I hung up.

Next I waited for Selma to come to the office, and when she did arrive, I let her ass have it next. She started putting everything on Mr. Lane as though she didn't know what was going on. "Selma, how the hell would you not know about this deal when your name is all over the offer? It even stated that if any dispute between you and me were to occur, then Mr. Lane would have the last word. What kind of fool do you think I am, Selma? Never mind, just pack your shit and leave my office today." I was pissed off but disappointed at the same time. Selma, I could see—but not Mr. Lane. Days went by, and Selma called to say she was very sorry and could she just explain what really happened. She wasn't a good agent, but I needed her, so I just listened. Finally, I hired her back for the sake of keeping the office open. I had my hands tied.

Peaches was not making my life any easier, and her mom was like the devil in drag. We were at her sister's house in Atlanta, and her mom and dad came to visit. I went over and tried to introduce myself to her mom with a friendly handshake. "Hi, how are you? My name is Stan, Peaches' boyfriend." She looked at me as my hand was extended and gave me the mean mug as though I was a rapist or something. She never extended her hand in return. I was thinking, *what kind of shit is this that I've gotten myself into? Who are these people and where the fuck did they come from?* Peaches never tried to come to my side. Instead, she just simply entertained her family as though we weren't even together. This was very strange shit in my mind because in all my life I had never been rejected by anyone's family, especially when I first met them. I realized right away that I was headed for some real problems.

My main problem was that my company was falling apart fast and I had no one to help me. Not only had I abandoned my company, but the reading that I had started to do had come to a complete stop. That was the one thing that had kept me balanced. My mind had been completely off the drugs, but now the street in me was starting to surface. I didn't have any money coming, but there was plenty going out. I never missed but two doctor visits during the pregnancy, and it was costing money every visit. The arguing continued and seemed to grow with every visit. Peaches was driving me crazy on top of it all. I was supportive of her, but she never gave me any support. I felt I still needed to be down for the baby. My sorry-ass father was never down for me, and I said I would never be him. So no matter what her family tried to do, I wasn't having any of that shit.

I owned six properties in Charlotte, and my sorry-ass tenants weren't paying the rent. This meant I had to pay, so I had to come up with something. My credit was messed up now, so I couldn't refinance my houses to get the money out. Life went from great to fucked up really fast. I thought I was doing the right thing by going into real estate, but it was turning into a nightmare. My man had flipped some homes and made lots of money. Some of the homes he had bought wholesale from the builder had gotten on average about fifty thousand per house at the table. This was why the Feds came to see him. He wasn't an agent, so they charged him with mortgage fraud. They froze his accounts and took $500,000 from him. When the redneck state board guy showed up, this was who he first asked about. This led me to think that they may be watching me also. I never knew that selling houses could put your ass in jail.

So now Peaches was being more of a pain in my ass more than anything else that was going on. Her parents were pressuring her, and so she passed it on to me. No matter how much she complained, I was still down. I continued to visit almost every weekend, yet Peaches' parents were still trying to convince her not to move with me in Charlotte. They wanted her to stay in Atlanta so they could control her life and have control of my newborn son. They were pissing me off more and more each second. Her mom was just mean as hell for no reason at all. She started trouble so I wouldn't have a good relationship with Peaches. She told Peaches not to visit me and that if I really loved her then I should always drive down to Atlanta. The crazy part about it was that Peaches went for everything her family said. Her mom also said not to have sex while she was pregnant because it would make her back hurt. What kind of dumb shit is that? Once again, Peaches went for that. So now I was running down to Atlanta and not getting any sex.

This was driving me totally crazy, but what could I do. She blamed it on her hormones. I was determined to have a family, so I put up with some shit that most men would have left alone. Instead of getting respect for what I was doing, Peaches and her family seemed to give me even more problems. They were determined to run me off, but I wasn't going to allow that to happen.

Peaches was torn between her family and me, and they knew that was the case, so they would continue to pull at her even while she was getting further along in her pregnancy. She was a graduate of FAMU, so every year they would drive to some big game in Florida. Peaches invited me to go so that we could make amends. That was the worst idea ever. As soon as I got to their home in Florida, they started drilling me and looking down on me like I was total trash. Peaches never once said anything in my defense, so it made me even more pissed off. We hadn't even made it to the game yet, but I wanted to go back home. The problem was I hadn't driven so I was stuck. I was trying hard not to curse her mother and father out, so mainly I stayed quiet. This turned out to be the worst trip of my entire life. The next day, we headed for the game and I rode with her mom and dad, which I hated from the start. Her father talked to me, but her mom was a true ass. We made a stop at Popeye's on the way down, so I tried to be nice to her mother and offered to buy her some food. She just looked at me and rolled her eyes like I had just cursed at her. She never said a single word, so I closed the door and went in and got my food. Now mind you, I was staying in the same room with them so I knew this wasn't going to get any better. Her father and I would drink Remy Martin together, so we had an okay relationship. Her mother hated that and quickly checked him, so he changed before the trip ended. I hadn't done anything but be supportive, so this was all strange to me. I bit my tongue so much; it had to have had a hole in it by then. We arrived at a rest stop, and they saw some old friends there. We all gathered around as they got reacquainted, but I was never introduced. It was as though I wasn't even a part of the group, so I went back to the car. This bullshit was getting old with me fast. I had never had to be so humble in my life. I had old girlfriends whose families still loved me, and yet my son's mother's family hated my very existence for no reason.

    Meanwhile, I couldn't maintain all of the properties, so two homes went into foreclosure. I was falling fast. I became very stressed out, not so much about the money or houses, but about my family. I really wanted to be able to raise my son and give him what I never had. I continued the visits, and we put Peaches' house on the market. That's when things started to come to light. Her family had put money into the house and her car, so they felt they should have complete control. I never knew that she wasn't independent until that point. She was a teacher, and I thought she was handling her business. Instead, her parents were handling her life. She allowed it so she could have the things they would buy her. In my mind, this was very childish and wrong on her parents' part. They meant well, but they had created a monster and were in fact being monsters. They wanted her to depend on them so they could control he life since they were old with not a damn thing else to do. The older sister was more outspoken, so she didn't allow them to control her life. I knew that I didn't fit into her family's world and they surely didn't fit into mine.

    That night, we got to the hotel and I had to sleep in the room with her dad, who snored like a damn bear, so I got no sleep at all. I wanted to catch a flight home, but Peaches got upset. She got mad at me because I asked her to say something to her family about the cold behavior. Instead she started giving me the cold shoulder along with them. This relationship was putting a strain on my life, to say the least. I couldn't stay focused because Peaches and her family were tearing me down emotionally. I decided to close my office and put an office back in my home. I was going crazy and started spending time alone. I had never been so unhappy in my whole life.

When Peaches was eight months pregnant, she decided to move to Charlotte with me to try to work on us. This made her family even more upset, so they pulled out all the tricks they had. I sold her house and it had lots of equity, so they drove up to Charlotte from Florida to demand the money back for the down payment on the house. This was only to try to keep her down and dependent on them. They also requested the car back they bought even though she made the monthly notes on it. I told Peaches to give back the money and the car because I had two cars. She gave back some of the money and kept the car. I started to hate them after that day because she was very upset and carrying my firstborn child. Until that day, I hadn't realized that after I stopped reading the Bible, all hell broke loose. It just came to me all at once. Satan had come in and was trying to destroy me and my seed. I was so stressed out, and I couldn't bring myself to read anymore. I was starting to get the "fuck it" attitude all over again.

Soon my son, Scooter, was born. Peaches had really good doctors, and the pregnancy had gone great. She had started having pains, so I stayed close to the house just in case her water broke. The next day, we had decided to go to Concord Mills to walk the baby down. We spent the whole day at the mall looking at baby clothes. The very same night, she started having really bad pain. I didn't realize what was going on at the time. She woke me up around 3:00 a.m. and asked me to call the doctor, but I was so sleepy I told her to lie back down. "Stan, I think it's time, so you need to wake up," she said.

"Come on, Peaches, go back to sleep. It's not time yet, so just hold my hand."

"Boy, wake up! It's time for real!" she yelled. It didn't do any good because I went back to sleep as she continued to squeeze my hand. Finally morning came and she called the doctor to say how far apart the pains were. The doctor told us to go to the hospital, and it finally hit me that I was going to be a daddy. I had waited thirty-seven years for this day. I drove to the hospital around noon as I alerted my family and friends. For some reason, I wasn't nervous at all. I was so excited, I told Peaches I had to go home to smoke one. She was so nervous that she didn't care. Her water hadn't broken, so my crew came to my house for some early celebrating. As soon as I returned to the hospital, the doctor told me that she broke Peaches' water and it was time. Now my nerves were suddenly bad. The moment I had waited on was finally here.

None of her family showed up for the delivery, but we held it down anyway. I was very nervous, but I didn't let anyone know. My mom and I were the only ones in the room during time of delivery, but she got light headed and was taken out. I thought for a moment that I would be next, but I hung in there like a soldier. The doctor prepped me on what to do, and I became a coach for Peaches. She counted to three, and I told her to push. "Ready— one, two, three, push." By the third time, I saw the top of my son's head showing. It was the most beautiful thing I had ever witnessed. The fourth push was the charm and out came my firstborn child at 7:44 p.m. on September 4, 2005. He slid out sideways and very fast, like he was shot out of a cannon. There he was—S.J.Long— right before my eyes. I always wondered what he would look like when he finally arrived. He was twenty-one inches long and six pounds, nine ounces. What a day that was for me. Scooter was red, almost white, with a head full of black hair. I looked at his hands and feet to see if they were okay. Then I thanked God for giving me a healthy baby boy. It had been placed in my spirit to name him Scooter from the start. I knew that he would be special. Peaches was happy finally and everything seemed to be fine. All of my problems seemed to disappear at least for the time being. All I could do was look at my newborn son. They kept Peaches for a few days and circumcised Scooter before he could come home.

Life seemed to smile at us for a while, and Scooter made everything okay. Peaches cried on the way home and told me that she was afraid. I tried to reassure her that we could do this together and this would be fine. For some reason, she didn't seem to be as happy as I was. We went home and looked at Scooter as though we had just bought a new Bentley. He would just cry and cry because we had to keep putting ointment on his private part. At one point, I looked over at Peaches and she was crying. "What's wrong with you, Peaches? Why are you crying?" I asked.

"Stan, I'm scared because I don't know what to do. I never had a baby before and what if I don't do the right thing. He's depending on me, and I'm afraid of being a mom." She started to cry even more, so I tried to encourage her by hugging her and telling her things would be fine and she would be a great mom.

"Baby, everything you do for the first time is a challenge, but with time it becomes second nature. I don't have any other children either, so we'll just have to work together." I didn't realize it at the time, but her family had placed fear in her by saying she couldn't do it by herself. This she confessed to me later. They were always being negative toward her and putting her down. None of them showed up for support during that time, but three days out of the hospital, and here they come.

They rang the doorbell, and truthfully I didn't want to let them in. Her mom and dad came in barely speaking to me and sat down with Scooter. Time went on, and her father and I got into a discussion about my plans and her mom started telling me that Peaches wasn't ready for a child. "Stan, Peaches can't even take care of herself, so how do you think she can handle a child? She doesn't know what to do with no baby," her mom said.

"Well, if you would give her a chance, then maybe she could do a lot of things. You haven't taught her to be independent; instead you and Jack have kept her dependent. I know she can do it, and I'm going to help her so she's not alone." Both of them became angry at my response, but I didn't give a damn because it was the truth. Peaches never opened her mouth, which was very strange to me.

Now it was her father's turn to chime in with his bullshit comments. Mind you we had just gotten home from the hospital three days before with the baby. "Well, Stan, real estate doesn't make money all the time, so what will you do when it's not making any money? My daughter needs to be taken care of, and I need to know that you'll do just that."

"I'm going to do fine, and if real estate goes bad, then I'll do something else. Why are you not being supportive about this? You seem to not want to let Peaches go, but she's a grown woman and not a little girl. You have to let go of her one day so she can have her own family," I stated.

"I don't have to do shit," he said as he angrily approached me. "She's my daughter, and I can do whatever I choose. I really want to knock the shit out of you is what I want to do," he shouted as he banged on my granite countertops.

I found myself in his face before I even realized that I had stood to my feet. "If you ever threaten me again in your life, they'll find you somewhere and nothing will be able to save your ass.

Now you've crossed the line with me, so get your ass out of my house and take your crazy-ass wife with you."

"No, wait, Stan, don't do it!" Peaches shouted. She knew what was coming next.

"Come on, let's go," her dad said angrily to her mom.

"Yeah, you need to get the hell out before I put my hands on you, and you're too old to handle that," I said. I knew this day would be a turning point for the worst, but I had had enough and didn't give a damn. Peaches was angry with me and sided with her dad. I wasn't a bit surprised. Her father tried to get her to leave with them. I could tell that she was confused, but I had gotten used to that. We had been to see a Christian counselor, and he basically told me that the first chance she got, she would flee. He advised me against getting married to her. This was different because normally they try to encourage marriage.

We didn't talk much after that, so I went upstairs to spend time with Scooter. I was very upset because they couldn't come to be supportive yet found the time to come and disturb my home. I never had been disrespectful up until that point. Even though I was viewed as a street person or hustler, I was always respectful to my elders, but this man came into my home with some bullshit. I could hear God talking to me more and more. He was trying to redirect my path, but I just wasn't listening. I told a few of my homeboys about the situation, and you already know what they wanted to do, kick his ass. I even had to tell one of them to leave from out front of my house. He came to make sure I was good. I wasn't used to being disrespected, and I wasn't ready to get used to it either. I did realize that these were her parents no matter how much I didn't like them at this point. Peaches felt she needed to take sides, and soon I found out just what side she was on.

A few weeks went by and she came to me saying she wanted to go visit her parents to let them bond with Scooter. We went back and forth about it for a few days, and finally I realized that she wasn't ready for a family at all, and in fact she was afraid. "You go ahead to Florida with Scooter and do what you have to, and I'll be right here." So she packed her clothes and my son's clothes and told me she would be back in a week. It didn't seem right to me, but I was tired of fussing with her. My mother was mad about it too, and we both realized that something was definitely wrong. Peaches said she was driving to her sister's house in Atlanta and her parents would pick her and Scooter up from there. The thought of my son going away after me seeing him for only three weeks was making me feeling sick, but I tried not to show it. The love that I felt for my son was like nothing I had ever felt before. I never knew you could love someone that much.

Something just wasn't right, but I couldn't say what it was at that time. Now when Peaches was around her family, she treated me differently, so I knew she wouldn't call much. I called her, and she was very short on the phone. Because of the fallout her father and I had, I couldn't call the house where my son was staying. This made matters worse because I could only talk if she called me. A week went by, and now Peaches was talking about staying there two weeks. Mind you, I hadn't spent but three weeks with him and she was gone. I started feeling like she wasn't coming back, so I started asking about clothes for him. She started making up shit and was being short, so I knew her mother or father must be around. The next day was a Wednesday, and Peaches called and my thoughts started coming true all in one moment. "Stan, I've been giving this situation a lot of thought and real estate doesn't make money all the time, so what's your plan B?" Now she had no job, no damn plan A or B, but this was her question. Actually it wasn't her question, but her parents' question because her dad had posed that to me at my house.

"Peaches, you're supposed to be my partner and my support, so why are you asking me this now? You never asked me anything until you got to Florida, and now all of a sudden you have doubt about me. I realize that you were never on my team from the start, so this shouldn't surprise me any. Your parents are filling you up with doubts about me and you're too blind to see it. Ask them what their plans were as teachers if they were to get fired. I can promise you that they had no plan. I'm a hustler, so something will work if real estate doesn't. I've made it just fine before real estate and I'll make it again."

"Well you should still have another plan just in case it doesn't work out. I don't feel comfortable in this situation at all," she said.

"Peaches, you have no plans at all and no job, but I don't down you for that. Even when I first met you, your teaching job was nothing because you didn't sign your contract and hadn't been placed anywhere. Did I ask you then about your plans or did I simply encourage you?" The next sound after that was a click in my ear. She hung up the phone, so I tried to call back but got no answer. I quickly realized that she and my only son were gone for good. After all the support and love I had given, this was my reward. I got tired of trying to call and getting no answer, so I decided to give it a break.

My main concern was Scooter. I had barely gotten a chance to see him and already he was out of my life. My first thought was of my father and how I felt growing up without him. I used to wonder how someone could have a child and not even be concerned about what was going on in their life. I had even tried to make things right with Peaches by giving her a ring when she was two months pregnant. When I gave her the ring, we were at Houston's in Atlanta. I even got down on one knee and the whole nine. Now that wasn't something I thought I would ever do. I went as far as to ask her father's permission to marry his daughter, which in my mind was very played out. I just wanted everything to be right. This was before all the bullshit had gone down and her dad was okay with me, or at least I thought he was. They were not happy when I hadn't given her a ring and then seemed to go even harder at me once I did. Peaches' attitude toward me after I gave her a ring seemed to get worse. I could not understand this shit to save my life. I sat and thought of all these things as I stared at the walls of an empty home. I remembered her telling me to take my ring and get ready to pay child support. She could be so cold that it was as if she never even knew me. I thought maybe this was karma for all of the things I had done to women in my past. How could someone you love treat you so badly?

Finally I just broke down into tears thinking of what was happening. I couldn't see my son, and that made me ache inside. I had never been depressed, so I couldn't tell if that was it or not, but what I did know was that the pain I was feeling was cutting me to the bone. It seemed like one long nightmare that wouldn't end. All the long trips and neglecting myself and my business to make a family, and as soon as my son was born, she took him far away from me. Peaches had planned this with her family after I kicked her parents out of my house. She led me to believe that she would return, but she knew that she wasn't coming back when she walked out the door. I began to develop a hate for her that was eating me up inside. I had forgiven her for things she had done to me time after time, but taking my only child away from me for no reason at all was out of the question.

I made arrangements to go down to Florida to see my son after a few months went by. I got a hotel room not far from where she was staying. I didn't have much choice because her family wouldn't allow me at their home. I got there on a Friday and waited for her to come to the hotel. After a few hours, she arrived and my eyes lit up to see Scooter, who for some reason was in nightclothes. Now I had sent a box of clothes with everything from jeans to shirts and more the week before. I tried not to mention it because I knew how Peaches would react. She said that she had to go to CVS to get some pampers. "Peaches, I just sent you a huge box of pampers at the bottom of the clothes."

"Stan, I didn't take anything out of the box. I haven't had time to do it yet," she said. "You can't be serious. After all the money I spent on clothes for him, you didn't even take them out of the box? How could you not care about what I sent to you for your child? You don't have to like me and that's fine, but this is not about me, it's about our son. You're not hurting me, but you're hurting him." As usual, she got mad and grabbed him up to leave. Something must have clicked after I mentioned that I drove all the way from North Carolina to Florida to see him and that she was going to just take him away because she didn't like what I said. She sat back down on the bed in silence. This girl knew how to piss me off. It seemed like she got a kick out of doing just that. I knew it was all for spite, so I tried not to feed into it. Scooter just sat and stared at me as though he knew I was his dad. The reason she chose that weekend for me to see him was because her family was out of town, so they wouldn't know I was there. The control they had over her was unimaginable. It was slowly wearing me down, and it was hard for me to keep hiding my feelings. It was the strangest situation I had ever heard of in my entire life. My family never treated her the way I was being treated.

Sunday came, and she still wouldn't let him stay the night with me. She said that he didn't know me like that. "How the fuck is he going to know me when you took him at three weeks old!" I yelled. The next thing I knew, they were headed out the hotel door. Once again, there I was looking like a damn fool.

I sometimes felt like God was punishing me for all the wrong that I had done because I could handle anything else that had gone my way from jail to shootings, but taking my only child away made me feel like I was dying a slow death. I had never loved like this before, so it was hard as hell to pull away. All I kept in mind is how my father wasn't around and how it made me feel growing up wondering why. I was determined that I wasn't going to give up on him no matter what Peaches tried to do. When she left, I can't lie, it angered me to the point of wanting to do something really bad to her and her crazy-ass family. Once again, I could hear God talking to me—*Get back into my word; I will make your crooked path straight.* My mind was so cloudy at the time that couldn't seem to pick up that Bible again. The night was so long because I couldn't bring myself to fall asleep. So I stayed up all night watching TV and wondering when I would see my son again.

Morning finally came and I was sleepy as hell, but my mind was on getting home, so I packed up bright and early and hit the highway. No matter what I tried to do, I couldn't shake the thought of my son. I called some friends on the way back to keep my mind occupied. There were only a few people I could talk to because I didn't believe in putting people in my business. Peaches tried calling me on the road, but I didn't have shit to say to her at that point. The highway seemed to get longer as I drove, but I needed that time to think of a plan. Finally after about ten hours, I was home. The next day, I called to set up a meeting with an attorney. I knew that Peaches was going to continue to play games, so I had to do something. I never believed in going to court, but I didn't have a choice at this point. A few days later, I went to see the best lawyer in Charlotte. It cost me $500 just to talk to her. I thought, *Damn, she better be good.* She advised me that my case would be hard because Peaches was in another state and had established residency. It was worth a shot, but she couldn't promise me. It would cost $5000 just to give it a try. Because he was so young and she claimed to be breast-feeding, my case would be difficult at best. This wasn't quite what I had in mind, so I told her I needed to think on it. I went home feeling like life was dealing me a fucked up hand.

    I didn't realize what was happening to me, but my hands would shake and pains started shooting down the left side of my neck. I would sit for hours staring at nothing and trying to collect my thoughts. I must have been having a nervous breakdown because this continued off and on for weeks. The pain came and went while my hand shook continuously for about a month. My life had gone to a place where I never thought I could be, I was falling behind on my bills, and my tenants weren't paying the mortgage on several of my properties. My friends would come by to check on me, but sometimes I pretended not to be home. They didn't need to see me in the state of mind I was in, and somehow I had to pull this shit together.

    After a few months, Peaches was blowing up my phone, but I was still ignoring her. This game had to end or I would let it take me down. I decided to pick myself up and get my life back together. I was free to start dating again, so I did just that. It was hard because all I thought of was my son and when I would see him again. One day, I met this really pretty, young lady name Bev. She was light skinned, which was new for me, because for some reason, I mainly had dated brown or dark women. It really didn't matter about the complexion as long as she was pretty and had some personality. I love a woman who can make me laugh and has great conversation. She had these eyes that changed colors and a pretty complexion. Most of all, she had pretty feet and hands. Don't ask why, but I love women with pretty feet. This went back to the third grade with Mrs. Billingsly. That's when I learned about my foot fetish.

    Anyway Bev and I started talking on the phone and she had a beautiful personality and she loved God. I connected with Bev right away. We even started going to church from time to time. She prayed for me once I told her about my son, and she wanted nothing but the best for me. This girl could cook her ass off too, so that was a plus. The real problem was the timing. I knew I wasn't ready to be in a relationship with her because I was just getting my mind back. Besides, I was newly single and starting to enjoy myself again. She was a buyer for a store called Belks, something on the lines of Nordstrom or Macy's. One thing I knew was that she really cared about me and she had my back. Bev wanted to settle down, but she also knew that I had other women; Sherril was one of those women. Now she was dark skinned and had a body like Beyoncé. Her hair was long and pretty, and she had brown eyes. Man, this girl was really something and she also loved God. It seemed like God was using them to bring me back to him and it was working in a strange way. Life is funny sometimes like that. You have your mind on one thing and God uses situations for something else. Finally I started reading again, but it was a serious battle in my mind. It felt like a tug-of-war every day. My situation with women was starting to get worse as I got my swagger back. My game face was back on, but my son never left my mind. Peaches and I started talking from time to time, but now I was completely over her, and she knew it. She wanted me back, but I had no plans of going down that road ever again. She would use Scooter to bait me into visiting her. It seemed to always be about her in her mind.

As I got back to reading more, life got much easier. My investment deals were picking up and soon I was back getting money in flipping houses. I would go to Atlanta from time to time to meet Peaches in order to see Scooter. He was getting big fast, and every time I left him, it broke me down. Peaches seemed to be bitter every time we would meet, so she wouldn't have much to say to me. I just ignored her and focused on my son. It was always a bittersweet trip because I hated having contact with my son's mom, but I loved to see my son and the smile on his face. Every time we talked on the phone, I would tell her to put Scooter on the phone and I would say my usual things to him to keep my voice in his mind. Somehow it always made me feel good. Peaches continued her mean, bitter attitude as though something was eating her up inside.

When Peaches and I met, I had been talking about God, and after a while, I allowed her to talk me out of God. Bev was quite the opposite. We started having Bible study, and she continued to try to talk me out of smoking weed. That was going to be hard because it was the one vice that seemed to keep me calm. I did finally stop selling weed, so that was a start. Remy Martin had started to make me sick, so I stopped drinking that too. It was small steps, but I was pulling it together slowly but surely.

Bev and I sat around reminiscing about my past and how God had saved me from death so many times. I told her of the time when my man Tye had gotten into a beef with some dudes and I didn't know about it. As we were gambling in the alley, they pulled up and leaned out of the window shooting. *Bang, bang,*

bang, bang, bang was all I heard, and as I looked up, I saw a guy leaning out of the car window pointing directly at me. For the first time my life, I heard bullets whizzing by my head as we ran behind the parked cars. The bullets then began hitting the cars that I hid behind, and I heard the car coming up into the parking lot. As I got up to run, the car was turning to leave the lot. Usually you don't hear bullets because if they get that close then you feel them. My life was spared once again. "Stan, you're so blessed just to be alive. Oh my God, I can't believe that you were even living that type of lifestyle from knowing you today. You're one of the nicest guys that I've ever met," Bev said. "You tell the story as if it happened to someone else and not you. It didn't scare you out of that lifestyle after that happened?"

I explained, "When you're into slanging drugs, you have to learn to accept what comes with it. If you get caught, you go to jail. If the young boys today only knew that they were playing a game with no rules. No rules mean no structure. It's a game that you can't win, but at that time, I didn't even realize that I was fighting a losing battle." As I said this to Bev, it seemed as though it had finally registered in my mind. I actually never really gave my life much thought until I started to read the word.

Although my life was changing for the better, my old habits still haunted me from time to time. Bev and I were getting closer, so I decided to take her to Maryland to see where I was really from and the area where I grew up and went to school. The trip was going fine at first. We stayed at the Marriott, and some friends came over to the hotel to visit. We started smoking weed and that's when things started going badly. As soon as they left, she started pressing me about smoking and why I hadn't totally stopped. "I thought you had given that up completely. Why did you lie and say you weren't going to smoke anymore?" she asked.

"Bev, first of all let's just get something straight, I'm a grown-ass man. You're not here to be my mother because I have one already. I'm out of town with some friends, and I'm chilling. Why are you so bent out of shape over me smoking a little weed?"

"Because you said you quit, and now you're smoking again. I guess you're not about your word." Now I found myself trying not to curse her ass out, so I tried to be quiet, but she just went on and on about it.

"Look, Bev, I don't have to explain what I do because I'm not even your man. I came to have a good time and that's what I plan to do. If you're going to try to control me, then we're not going to make it too long," I said. She became quiet, and I thought that was the end of it, but I was wrong. About twenty minutes later, she started pretending to be sick. She was faking like she was throwing up, but I could tell it was fake. The shit got on my nerves so bad that I left the next morning and headed straight back to Charlotte.

The next thing I know, I got a call from my mother while in the car. "Stan. I thought you said you weren't still smoking drugs? Bev called me all upset last night to say you were smoking."

"Bev did what? Mom, tell me you're playing. As a matter of fact, let me give you a call later." I hung up and said to Bev, "You know what, when we get home, don't call my phone ever again in your life. You've crossed the line with this shit, why the hell do you have my mother all in my business? I'm not a damn child!"

"Stan, I was only trying to look out for you, but okay that's fine, just drop me off." So needless to say, it was a long, silent trip home. I really wasn't smoking much weed anymore, but who was she to put my mother in my business? I had never had anything like that happen to me. We finally made it home and I dropped her off. She called me the next day, but the conversation was limited. We saw each other a few times after that, but it just wasn't the same, so I let it go. Meanwhile, Peaches was starting to call me more. She was talking like she had some sense all of a sudden. I asked her what was with her new attitude, and she said she had been reading the word. "You've been doing what? Say that again so I can make sure I heard you correctly. I thought you said that you had been reading the word."

"Stop playing, Stan. I'm serious. I've been doing a lot of soul searching and you've been right. I should act more like an adult and make my own decisions. My parents have controlled me all of my life, but I have allowed that to happen. If only I would have stood up for myself, then maybe things would be different. I hate being away from you because I realize now that you are a very good person but I let my family mess things up for us. I'm in a dark place now, so reading has been helping me. I just want to say sorry for everything." I was totally speechless. She had fooled me so many times; I didn't really know what to think. One thing I did know was that even after all the shit, I still loved her. She had given me my only child in the world. "Peaches, that's a great thing, and I'm glad you finally woke up. Maybe now we can work on being friends for my son. He really is going to need both of us." She agreed, and we ended the conversation shortly after. Deep inside, I wasn't trying to go back to her because we had been through too much. At the same time, I wanted a family and I longed to be with my son. I tried to get back to my Bible to keep my mind straight. The house wasn't the same being in it alone.

I started back with the different women to keep me from feeling down. None of them kept my mind from my son. Meanwhile, my mother's friend from Baltimore wanted a house in Charlotte. They had known each other forever. I found her a house in Lake Norman, which is fifteen minutes outside of Charlotte. She came down with her daughter, Nikki, who was very sexy. I hadn't seen her since we were kids. We all met up for dinner, and all I saw were legs and feet step out of the truck. There was something about her that drew me right away. She was funny and had a really nice personality. I knew we could only be friends, but damn.

After her mom purchased a house, I took Nikki out to celebrate. That's when we really got to know each other better. She told me about her crazy-ass boyfriend, and we laughed and had a good time. I took her home and didn't hear anything from her for a while. One day, she called and said she was at the hairdresser and wanted to know what I was doing. The timing was perfect, so I drove to her and we sat in my car and talked. "Do you want to hang out for a while?" I asked.

"Sure," she said. "What did you have in mind?"

"We can go to my house and get a paper, maybe see a movie."

"That's cool, let me call and check on my boys." So we ended up at my house and that's when things changed. We ended up getting some wine and skipping the movie. She was fun, so we had a great time just talking and laughing. Nikki ended up staying overnight, and I didn't even try her. Okay, I'm lying, but she didn't go for it. At least not that night. Morning came and I felt a leg on my leg. After that, well, I'll just say we had a great time. We became close extremely fast and I saw her almost every day. Meanwhile, Peaches would blow my phone up until I cut the ringer off. It seemed like every time I got close with someone, she could smell it from Florida. Business was going well and life was fun again. Somehow from long distance Peaches could sense it. Nikki and I were spending more and more time together. I was actually falling for her, but I didn't let on to her.

One day in the car, Nikki looked at me and told me she loved me. Like a punk, I responded right back. It's like I couldn't hold back; my feelings for her had begun to take over. This wasn't supposed to happen to me. *Hell no, Stan, you have to shake this off.* Her boyfriend had gotten arrested shortly after she moved to Charlotte, so he was quickly out of the picture. We began to hang out all the time and do things like go to basketball games and other functions. My homeboys would say, "Stan, what's up with your super model?" That's what I would call her. Nikki was also the type of girl that didn't mind getting her hands dirty. She would come over in sweat pants and a T-shirt and wash her car, then take a shower and put on a fly dress and some pumps. We had cookouts at my house a lot, and many people would show up and we would have a ball. Most of the time, it was during a fight or a basketball game. Life was really good and so was business.

Peaches and I talked on a regular basis, but I wasn't trying to get back with her. I was enjoying my life and didn't want to go backwards. I must admit that she was talking like she had some sense finally, but she had stabbed me in the back so many times before that I couldn't allow myself to go back to her. Deep down inside, I wanted my family, but she had made my life too difficult to even consider going back.

Nikki was becoming more and more attached as the days went by. She started putting more demands on me, and I wasn't having all that. She started staying over almost every night. I wasn't ready for a relationship just yet. Every girl that I got involved with seemed to try to make me her man. Nikki was cool, but she also had some issues. Her two sons were cool too, but that wasn't going to work—me raising two boys with another woman and not seeing my own. I tried to pull away from Nikki and things got worse. She complained to me about me not wanting to spend time and she also threw little hints about moving into my house. Now that was a hell to the no.

Peaches came up a few weeks later to visit and things went okay. I must admit that I was happy to see her, but even more happy to see my son. I felt strange having her around; after all, she had up and left me and took my only son. I tried to put things behind me, but that was a tough pill to swallow for anyone who truly loves their child. We talked a lot, but it seemed as though we were on different pages. I felt like a man trying to date a little girl. My feelings had changed for Peaches, so I didn't look at her the same. Nikki was having a hard time with the fact that Peaches was staying at my house. She expected me to make her get a room, which was some bull shit because my son was the main reason she came and he wasn't about to stay at no damn hotel. She started bitching and complaining about it to the point that I had to not answer her calls. I knew at that point that it was not going to last much longer. I could tell that Peaches had changed for the better, but she still had some issues that were a problem. She tried to hide it, but in the two weeks that she stayed, they started coming out.

After two weeks, Peaches returned with Scooter to Florida and we continued to talk on the phone but mostly about my son. Nikki called and wanted to talk about us. "Stan, I think you and I need to talk face-to-face about some things. I didn't hear from you the whole time your son's mom was in town. You need to tell me what the fuck is going on with you," she said. About an hour later, she came over and we talked about us. "So how come you couldn't call me or answer my calls while your son's mom was here? I thought it was just about your son, Stan."

"It is, and that's why I didn't call you—because I was spending my time with him. He's young, so his mom is involved until I get to know him and he gets comfortable with me. You know damn well I haven't seen him since I don't know how long and I'm not letting anything come between that. Plus, Nikki, you're not my girl, so why are you talking crazy like that's what it is?"

"Okay, so you fuck me when you want and whatever else, and then it's fuck me. I see what you want, some call-up pussy. I'm too old to be that, so maybe you need to get back with your baby's mother, because I'm not going to play second to anyone."

"You're right, you don't have to, but you're not going to stress me about this. We need to just cut this shit short now and keep it moving!" The next thing I knew, Nikki was crying her eyes out and storming out of the house. I felt bad because she was a good girl, but she was getting too close too fast. My hands were tied, and I was trying to make a relationship with my son, not his mom.

I didn't hear from Nikki for about a week. Peaches was still calling and trying to make up. She called out of the blue and said that God asked her to bring Scooter back to me. She was crying and being very apologetic, yet something inside me was saying don't do it. On the other hand, I was missing my son so badly that it seemed like a good idea. We talked about it for days and then I agreed to let her move back in with me. I had mixed emotions about it, but I was willing to do anything to see my son every day and get to know him better. Peaches knew how much I loved my son, so she played games with him to keep me around. It's like she didn't want me, but she didn't want anyone else to have me either. I told myself that I would give this one more try and after that I was not dealing with her ever again.

Nikki called to say she wasn't coming over again. She told me she was moving on and that she was very hurt. I told her that I wished things could have been different because I really enjoyed her company but the timing was bad. Peaches finally came back, and soon after she did, the real her started to come out all over again. I knew I should have listened to myself.

Peaches bought her ass back bitterer than ever. I was determined to make the best of it because in my heart I knew that this was going to be my last try. They say if you don't give something 100 percent effort, then how can you say you really tried. The bottom line was that we were on two different pages from the very start. Actually, I should say two different books. I was an independent thinker while she was pampered and sheltered all of her life. They say opposites attract, but in this case, we were too opposite, so we pulled on each other. This quickly became a match made in hell.

Now mind you, we had already spent the last few months not even talking, so I thought maybe things would be different this time since she had said God told her to return. I knew in my heart that no matter how much you go left, God could change a person's heart. I had gotten my mentality together and was making money again, and as soon as Peaches came back, it all came to an end again. We all know that you can only do what you can think of, and when you can't think, then you can't do anything. Everything starts with your mind. Now don't get me wrong, we did have some good days, but the bad certainly outweighed the good. Some days she would walk by and not say anything at all to me. Mind you, she was living in my damn house. All I could think of was that I had given up dating and happiness for the same shit I had left long behind. I realized that the way she was had been passed down from her mom. Her mom hadn't dealt with her past hurts, so she was a very bitter woman. I thought to myself, *there's no way I can live with this shit for the rest of my life. I'm a positive person, so the negative spirit is not going to mix with what I'm trying to do.*

We constantly got into heated arguments, and it was in front of my son. I started to reflect on my childhood and what my father had done to my mother in front of me and how it made me feel. Plus, on top of all the drama, she wasn't involved with anything positive that I was trying to accomplish. There were never any words of encouragement or advice. I thought of how my father would beat my mother down or curse her out and I decided that even though this would temporarily separate me from Scooter, it was the best thing for me to do. When you get a relationship with God, you realize that he has a sense of humor with his children. I sat down and told Peaches that we were no good for each other and we needed to part ways. She agreed, and so I walked off after we made that decision. About five minutes later as I left my office and entered my bedroom, she came in behind me saying, "I hear you, God, I hear you, God." Soon after that, she started speaking in tongues and shaking really badly, and the Holy Spirit came on her right in front of my eyes. It was something I had never witnessed before. She went into singing loudly, saying, "Thank you, Jesus, thank you, Jesus." Then her voice got deeper as the shaking got worse.

    I won't go into all the details, but maybe twenty minutes into this, God spoke to me saying, "Put your hand on her forehead," and so I did that. Then for some reason, I started saying, "Come out of her, come out of her." I'm not going to lie; I wasn't quite ready for the thing that happened next. All of a sudden, she made many faces and it seemed as though stuff was being pulled out of her. I can't explain the work of the Lord, but it was something that only the believer could wrap his or her mind around. Now this went on for about forty-five minutes until she no longer had the strength to stand. I sat her on the bed, and she popped right back up and started thanking God again. Her hair was sweated out, and so I went to get her a wet, cold rag. She finally calmed down, and before I realized it, we had let time go by and were late picking up Scooter from daycare. She made it to the daycare with a blank stare on her face. I didn't quite know what to make of the situation, so I said nothing. That was a day I'll never forget.

    We talked about it much later and decided that maybe we shouldn't give up so quickly. It was like divine intervention. She was a different person after that, for a while at least. We started to get along much better and we talked about the Lord more. A few months went by and then we stopped reading the Bible and things went right back to the way they had been. Finally it was coming down to the fact that it just wasn't working at all. This time I knew it was over. She started looking for a teaching job back in Atlanta, and her family was back in her ear again. I totally let it go this time. I knew I had to get my focus back. She was focused on her, and I was focused on myself, and deep inside I knew it was the best thing for us. We all know that you need chemistry to stay together, and that was something we never developed.

    After a few weeks, she asked if I would keep Scooter for a while; she wanted to stay with her sister in Atlanta to get a job. That was a question I had prayed for, so my answer was, "Hell yeah, I'll keep him forever." She finally moved to Atlanta with her sister and found a good teaching job. Scooter stayed with me for three months while she tried to find a place. This was great for me because it was a true bonding period. School was about to start and Peaches found a place, so she wanted Scooter to come to Atlanta to find a daycare. I helped her with the down payment so I could have a place to come and spend time with my son. Her sister and I weren't too cool, so I hated visiting them at her house. She found a nice townhome in a gated community that was nice. "Stan, I know we didn't make it together, but I want you to know that you're welcome to come and see Scooter anytime, and I'll never keep him from you again," she said. "Good because it not only hurts me, but more so it hurts him in the long run. Scooter deserves two parents who can at least get along." She agreed, and so we were off to a great start this time. Peaches kept her word, and I finally took him down to Atlanta to stay. It was the hardest thing to do because I was just getting to really know him. Remember, she took him and left me after he was only three weeks old. She didn't return him until he was almost one year old. She had a lot of things she had to deal with growing up. Your childhood has everything to do with your future. She had always been compared to her older sister. They said she was stupid and couldn't take care of herself or a baby. They always put her down, and that plays a part on who you can become. I never thought of any of this until this point. I was watching her grow up right before my eyes.

    I must admit that I myself didn't trust her ability to handle him alone because she had fed into what her parents said about her. She was weak-minded and lacked confidence, making it hard for me to believe in her. Anyway, time went on and she seemed to be handling things just fine. I started going back and forth to Atlanta to see my son, and my relationship was good with Peaches finally. I was proud of her because she was proving her family wrong.

    I loved Atlanta anyway, so I was considering moving down to be closer to Scooter. My bills were piling up because now real estate was at an all-time low and I didn't know what to do. I had gotten away from reading again and was back smoking weed and hanging out. CIAA was coming to Charlotte soon, and people were coming into town from everywhere. I was trying to throw some parties to make extra money. I had been doing well staying out of trouble for years and I was trying not to go down the wrong path again, but my pockets were getting low and my connect was on speed dial. Jay-Z and Mary J were coming to the Greensboro Coliseum, and I had great seats, so I looked forward to going to clear my head and have some fun.

Finally the show date came, and I headed to the corner store for some blunts for that night. My homeboy and I went to the store, got blunts, and then headed home. We stopped at a red light outside the store and all of a sudden, "Watch out, watch out!" my man said. As I looked around to my right, there was a jeep coming right at us. He swerved and almost hit me head-on. I was pissed off, so I turned around and went into the gas station behind him. By the time I got there, he was out the jeep and in the store buying beer. My man and I got out and went into the crowded store to approach him. He was a young, white guy about six feet tall.

"You didn't see that red light you ran when you almost hit us head-on?" I asked him.

"I had to get some fucking gas!" he shouted.

"So you're going to kill someone to get gas? Is that what you're saying?" I asked him. "Man, fuck it, what do you want to do?" he said as he put the beer down. Now at this point, he left me know room; before I knew anything, I was punching him in his jaw. He fell back and then came at me, but he didn't know that my fight game is tight. He found out quickly. I hit him with so many combos till he hit the floor. My man assisted with some blows also, but not many. Then I lost it and stomped him out and left him on the floor. I kicked him until my right toe was broken. We quickly got in my truck and pulled off, leaving him in the store in the fetal position.

"Damn, hommie, all I wanted was some blunts for the show," I said.

"I know," my man said, "but that motherfucker was drunk and he asked for that ass kicking."

"Yeah, you're right about that shit." So we went back to my house, and in the next half hour, I heard a banging on my front door.

"It's the police," my man said.

"Damn, they wrote my tag down and called on us. Don't answer the door," I said quietly. Finally he left his card in my door and then left. I grabbed some clothes and the card and left to go call my lawyer. I then called the officer back and he was a straight redneck. "Ahh, Dan, Stan, or whatever your name is, you need to come down to the station and give me a statement."

"I'm charged with a crime?" I asked.

"No, not as of yet," he said with a country twang.

"Well I'm not coming down to give anything. I don't make statements without my lawyer, and if I'm not charged, then I'm not going to come down," I said.

"Well, son, why don't you tell me exactly what happened or we'll have to take out a warrant because the young man you hit is in the hospital and he pressed charges on you."

"I'll have my lawyer call you because I don't give statements, sir." I went on to the show that night with a broken toe and all. The next day, I turned myself in with my lawyer, and they let me go. Then they came back with a warrant, so I had to turn myself in again the next day. My lawyer got me right back out, but it was far from over. They charged me with assault with a deadly weapon. I didn't know what to think, but my lawyer said they were trying to give me some time. Now Mint Hill was a redneck town, so it didn't surprise me any. My lawyer said that I could get probation if I said I was leaving the city. Atlanta came to my mind right away. I agreed to say I would move, and God got me one year of probation. They wanted me to tell on my man, but I don't snitch, so those rednecks put the shit on the news three weeks later to try and get someone to tell. No one told, but the whole city was calling me now, including my investors. The shit was starting to stink. I stayed awhile, and CIAA came up. My man's sister Rasheeda came up from Atlanta for the parties. I had dated her some fifteen years ago and we were still friends. She had given me the Bible at my store in Maryland. She was all happy about some company that was paying her well. She told me about it, but I was half listening because I had other shit on my mind at that time.

So weeks went by and I went to Atlanta for my son. Rasheeda called me to go to a meeting with her. I went, and it was the start of a new life for me. They were getting paid well, and it was health and Wellness Company. The compensation plan was so crazy, I signed on the next day. I told you God has a sense of humor. Atlanta was the second city the company came to, so the timing was perfect. People were making $100,000 a month in this business. That was dope money in my mind. The timing couldn't have been better. Peaches allowed me to stay with her so I could go to more meetings. Now things were starting to come together on a whole other level. God had placed me in a business with an opportunity to make $50,000–$100,000 a month. They did no background checks or credit checks. This was heaven sent because my credit was bad, my criminal record showed me on probation for assault, and I was self-employed for so long, no one would give me a job. God showed me a new plan, so I took off in the company and started making money right away. Meanwhile, Peaches and I were doing okay because we weren't together, so there was nothing to fuss about anymore. Also I had this great book coming out and I just knew it would become a bestseller. I had even titled three more books as I was writing the first one. While in North

Carolina, I had become co-owner of a music studio and we were in the process of getting clearance for a Motown sample, which is very hard to do because Motown does not usually allow sampling of their music.

    I met a guy named Harvey Fuqua. He was a cool dude around seventy years old with a swagger on a thousand. We sat and talked because he knew my man Mike who owned the studio. Mike introduced us, and so I talked to him about my book. He told me he loved my story and he would like to put it on film. I didn't know who he was at that time, but he told me that he was the man who introduced Marvin Gaye to Mr. Barry Gordy. He had a group called the Moon Glows back in the day, and Marvin would sit in and sing for them from time to time. Now this man went back to when they were called Hitsville, USA. I knew nothing about it because I was too young. Then he said, "Do you know that my nephew is Antwone Fuqua who directed *Training Day*? Now the crazy part was that my accountant also was great friends with Denzel Washington because his wife and Denzel's wife went to school together." I saw then that God was directing me to tell my story to the world.

    Things were getting better all the time, and my relationship with my son was great. Peaches had started really growing up now and being more independent. She wasn't letting her parents dictate her life anymore. Although I still didn't want to get back with her, at least I could respect her. We started to hang out some in Atlanta and take Scooter out to parks and movies. This was good for him to finally see us getting along. She had a long way to go, but things were looking much better.

    I still had my house in Charlotte, but it was on the market. Real estate was still at an all-time low, and anyone who was in the game was totally broke—mortgage brokers, builders, developers, and so on. I never thought I'd see the day a developer would be broke. The economy was taking a hit for the worse because Bush had bankrupted the country. I knew it was based all on New World Order. I was into that kind of thing. I had read lots of books about it years before. One in particular was *Behold a Pale Horse* by William Cooper who is a hero to America. Anyway, we were in a depression, but everyone called it a recession. In spite of it all, God was blessing me still. We had just elected the first black president in the United States, President Barack Obama. I knew that wasn't going to change America, but at least blacks had finally made it to the top. It was a shift in time for blacks. Every one could feel it even in the midst of very bad times. Wars were going on and corruption was being exposed. Life kind of felt good and bad at the same time.

    I went back and forth to Charlotte, trying to sell my last home. My man Bump from DC had moved to Charlotte and he was having a fortieth birthday party. People flew in from Miami, Houston, DC, California, and many other places for his party. He was a very popular guy in DC, and I found out that night that it wasn't limited to just DC. Bump was looked at as a fun guy with lots of cash and he knew how to party. We started at a high-end hotel in Charlotte, and he had two suites reserved, one to eat and drink in and the other for him and his wife. Then a shuttle bus came to pick us up and took us to and from the club. Now I can't lie, I've been to many parties, but this one was off the chain. My man Adolf owned the club, so we were all VIP. We all partied like rock stars that night, but I started to notice that this shit was far behind me now.

    After I started to get more into the word, my life started changing as to what was important. Don't get me wrong, I loved to have a good time, but my life was changing slowly in front of my eyes. The things that held value at one point didn't mean much at all anymore. I still wore Gucci, Prada, True Religion, etc., but it wasn't a must have. I was starting to see things on another level now and it felt good to me. I was at peace with myself for the first time in my life. I found God coming out of my mouth on an everyday basis. Secret books that people didn't and don't know exist were being handed to me from out of nowhere. This health and wellness business was placing me into arenas that I never dreamed of. Peaches was changing just by seeing my growth. Now don't get me wrong, I wasn't religious by far, just a truth seeker. I found myself falling in love with the Nameless One. He was talking me places in life that I knew I would never have gone on my own. I had become a writer and didn't even know it. He was making me into a motivational speaker at the same time because of my position in the company.

Peaches and I couldn't be together because I wasn't willing to give her my heart again, but it was good just to get along with her. We had become great friends and it was great for Scooter. Life had taken a turn for the good, and finally I wasn't doing anything illegal. I had finally gotten my credit straight and started to look for my own place in Atlanta. Peaches wasn't happy about it at all. Seems as though reality had set in and she didn't want to let go.

    One day I was coming out of the shower, and Peaches was standing in the doorway. "Stan, I want you to pack your shit and leave now! You can't stay in my house anymore!" Peaches screamed.

    "What are you talking about? I'm supposed to be leaving at the end of the month. I thought we were cool, so what's this all about?" I asked.

"I went in your phone while you were taking a shower, and I don't like what I saw. You can just go stay with that bitch Nae!" she yelled.

"Peaches, we're just friends, so why are you going through my phone? I have never bothered your phone."

"I don't want to hear that shit. Just pack your little bags and get the fuck out of my house now."

"So you want to just put me in the streets all in one day because of a text in my phone? See this is that bipolar shit you do, and this is exactly why I'm moving out. Why can't you give me until the end of the month as planned? Shit, today is the eighteenth anyway."

As I said that, I reached for her phone that I paid the bill for and took it off of the dresser.

"Give me my damn phone!" she yelled as she grabbed me and tried to fight me.

"No, let me see who you're calling since you're so worried about my shit. I already know about Tom and your other dude. And I never gave a damn," I said as we tussled over the phone. After the phone broke, the tussling came to an end. "I can't believe this bullshit. What the hell is wrong with you?" I asked as I got dressed.

So she grabbed my son, who was crying, and left the house. I finished getting dressed for traffic court and left out. Court was cancelled for the MLK holiday, so I met with Nae to get something to eat. After eating and talking with Nae, I went back to Peaches's place to get my things. When I arrived, the police were in the driveway. As soon as I got out of the truck, the officers approached and asked me to place my hands behind my back. This was the last thing that I expected at this stage in my life. Everything was starting to look up and then this happens.

As the officers took me away, Peaches yelled, "You will never see your son again! I promise you that!"

That day began the fight of my life. I got out of jail the next day, and now it was time to pay lawyers once again. Months later, I beat the charges, but I had to take anger management classes. That was the least of my worries. My son was out of my life again, but this time it seemed to be a permanent situation. I hired a lawyer for family law, and now it was time to fight. Peaches let Scooter call me for about a month, and after that I didn't hear from him. She then took out a restraining order to stop me from trying to see him. That's the worst thing that could happen to a man.

So as I suit up in Hugo Boss to get ready for court, and I think of all the things a man could find himself in court for; this one just never came to mind. They say God doesn't put more on you than you can handle. I try to hold on to that thought as I wonder how I got here. Maybe this is karma for all the wrong I've done. Maybe womanizing and living selfishly has finally caught up with me. All I know for sure is that I wouldn't wish this on anyone, not even my worst enemy. They say lots of men find themselves in this position, but I never dreamed it would be me. This time I feel like I'm in mental prison before even arriving at court. To make matters worse, my lawyer told me that the judge is a real bitch.

The thought of taking the biggest loss of my life seemed to consume me daily. My friends and family all tried to keep me in good spirits, but even they realized that this time I might have stepped in some real shit. I guess I could say that only God could save me from what I was about to face. I'm a real soldier, so I was staying strong, but I could see how it could break a man down.

About nine months went by and still no word from Scooter. It felt like I was missing a limb. My lawyer finally got me visitation rights and after lots of praying, my son was finally dropped off to me, he jumped out of the car and ran into my arms, I was so emotional it brought me tears. I drove him home and we talked the entire ride. He had grown so much it was amazing, his speech was even better than I had remembered. I could tell that he had missed me as much as I'd missed him.

    Finally we reached my new condo and I immediately took him to his room. He was thrilled about it and he turned around and gave me a high five. That was our sign that things were all good, I showed him his new clothes and then we sat and just talked, it was difficult for me to hold back the tears .The next day we went to look at furniture for him and I decided to let him choose whatever he liked. This was the start of the best days of my life.

    After a long battle in court, I was granted joint custody of my son. Peaches and I never worked out our differences, and yet somehow my life seems to be much better.

    So here I stand in this mirror as a man who came from drug dealing and being a gangster to a real man with knowledge of self—a writer, motivational speaker, independent filmmaker, and a successful businessman. This is what happens when you put your faith in the Nameless One.